GLAD ENCOUNTER

ABOUT THE AUTHOR

George Appleton was for nineteen years a missionary with the S.P.G. in Burma, where he came to a
deep reverence for the person of the Buddha and
a sincere admiration for the moral teaching of
Buddhism. After returning to Britain he served
for eight years as a Secretary of the Conference of
British Missionary Societies. He is now Rector of
S. Botolph's Church, Aldgate, in the City of London,
where he is trying to get into friendly touch with
people of other faiths. Author of *In His Name, The
Christian Approach to the Buddhist.*

GLAD ENCOUNTER

Jesus Christ and the Living Faiths of Men

by

GEORGE APPLETON

LONDON
EDINBURGH HOUSE PRESS
2 EATON GATE, S.W.I

© George Appleton 1959

First published 1959

MADE AND PRINTED IN GREAT BRITAIN BY
MORRISON AND GIBB LIMITED, LONDON AND EDINBURGH

CONTENTS

ACKNOWLEDGMENTS

WE are deeply grateful to all the authors and publishers, who have given us permission to use the extracts from their books. Full details of the sources of the quotations used in the text of the book are given in the footnotes. The quotation from *The Everlasting Mercy* is reproduced by permission of the Society of Authors, and Dr. John Masefield, O.M., also by arrangement with the Macmillan Company, New York. The lines from *Gitanjali* are printed by permission of the Trustees of Rabindranath Tagore and Macmillan and Co. Ltd., London. The extract from the Prayer Book as proposed in 1928 is printed with the permission of the Holders of the Copyright.

The prayers at the end of each chapter are taken from the following sources and again we are grateful to all concerned for permission to use them here. On pp. 12, 26, 39 and 50 the prayers by E. Milner-White are from *My God, My Glory* and those on pp. 26 (third) and 85 by the same author are from *A Procession of Passion Prayers*, both books published by the S.P.C.K. ; p. 12, *The London Service Book*, is edited by G. W. Briggs, Oxford University Press ; p. 26, the prayer by Dr. W. R. Matthews is from his book, *Seven Words*, Hodder & Stoughton Ltd. ; p. 40, Olive Wyon's prayer is from *Praying for Unity, II*, Edinburgh House Press; p. 62, E. Milner-White's prayer is from *After the Third Collect*, A. R. Mowbray and Co. Ltd. ; p. 74, the author's first prayer is from *In His Name*, Macmillan and Co. Ltd. and Edinburgh House Press ; p. 86, William Temple's prayer is from *William Temple and his Message* by Canon A. E. Baker, published by Penguin Books Ltd., and is reproduced with the permission of Mrs. Temple ; on the same page the extract from the Nestorian Liturgy is taken from *Daily Prayer*, edited by E. Milner-White and G. W. Briggs, and published by Oxford University Press.

FOREWORD

THE revival of the ancient religions of Asia has brought them into encounter with Christianity as never before. I believe that Christians should accept this new encounter gladly and eagerly, for it gives them the opportunity of showing that Jesus Christ is relevant to all religions.

Men everywhere are interested in Jesus Christ. Many Hindus would accept him as an incarnation of God. Many Buddhists would give him a place in the succession of Buddhas. The Qur'an of the Muslims speaks of him as a prophet and messenger sent by God, and as the Word of God. Many Jews are prepared to regard him as the greatest of Jews ; sternly orthodox Jews completely reject him still, possibly because nineteen centuries of bitter experience of Christendom come between him and them.

Beginning with the great doctrines of the Christian faith this book tries to interpret Jesus Christ as good news to men of other religions. I believe that the Eternal Christ is always at work lighting every man, the source of all truth, goodness and love. Acceptance of this belief involves a new, welcoming attitude to men of other faiths, which will recognize that God is at work in their religions, preparing them for the glad encounter with Jesus Christ as Lord and Saviour.

G. A.

CHAPTER I

HE WHO IS

In the early years of his missionary service the writer was taking a class in a village mission school in the Irrawaddy Delta in Burma. It was a scripture lesson, and his aim was to bring out the point that if we want to know what God is like, we have only to look at Jesus. Wishing to stimulate the imagination of the class, he began with the question, ' What is God like ? ' to be disconcerted by the prompt and truculent reply from a Buddhist boy, ' There isn't any God.'

Thirty years later, teaching in a secondary modern school which draws most of its pupils from East London, the same innocent was talking to the senior class about God's purpose of love and blessing for all nations being fulfilled through Christ and his Church. Towards the end of the lesson he invited discussion, and was greeted by the immediate and radical question, ' How d'you know there is a God ? Our dad says there isn't one.'

In presenting the Gospel to the world today Christians can take nothing for granted. Here in the west there has been a marked falling away from the Christian faith : the B.B.C. in a recent project of listener research estimated that only fifteen per cent of the population in this country committed themselves to full membership of the Church. Christian visitors from countries overseas, whose churches have been planted largely by the missionary movement from this country. have expressed their surprise and dismay that many of our churches are so poorly attended. Overseas, the revival in the non-Christian religions and their missionary activity are challenging the Christian faith as never before. East and west alike, we are being called to give reasons for the faith that is in us, to relate it to world conditions, and to present it in a way that shall prove it to be good news in terms of the other religions.

This book is written for Christians in Britain, asking them to re-think their own faith from the beginning, so that they may be able to give a new and more compelling witness to non-Christians through a new understanding of their situation. Only as we ourselves go through the doubts, questions and denials of other people, as well as their beliefs, aspirations and hopes, can we confirm our own faith and relate it to other people in terms of their own searching, thinking, and experience.

The existence of God is the most important question of all, and Christians must not evade the difficulties involved in it, whether they are raised by people educated in a scientific background, or Southern Buddhists who assume that there is no Supreme Being as easily and naturally as Christians assume that there is, or Communists who believe that all religion is a hang-over from a superstitious past, or by agnostics who say that they do not know whether there is a God or not, and in most cases do not consider the question a vital one.

Hindus form another class of people, for to the Hindu God is impersonal. Brahman the creator is ' beyond the reach of thought and voice '. He is unknowable, and therefore all religions are but human attempts to get to know him, all more or less true, none more true than others. In this conception there can be no final religion ; Christ is reverenced, but as one divine being among many others. The Hindu, while giving Christianity a place within its temple of religions, refuses to give it that uniquely supreme place that Christians claim for it.

S. Paul at Athens found an altar with the inscription, ' To an unknown God '. It is just possible that the Athenian, who erected the altar with this dedication, wanted to be on the safe side in leaving unworshipped no god, who at some later reckoning might punish such an omission. It is more likely that he thought of God as unknown, and that the inscription really meant, ' To the unknowable God '. For even Plato the wisest of the Greek thinkers, could write, ' The Maker of this universe is hard to find ; nor if he were found could he be declared to all men.'

The Bible would agree that man in his own wisdom and power cannot know God. ' Canst thou by searching find out God ? ' asks Zophar of the stricken Job, while S. Paul in his first letter to Timothy speaks of the blessed God ' who only hath immortality, dwelling in light unapproachable ; whom no man hath seen, nor can see.'

Yet the theme of the Bible is that God is a God who is always making himself known to men. God is a God who speaks. If he were not so, it would be impossible for men to know him ; he would be completely remote, known only to himself. The Bible is the record of God's revelation of himself to men. It never argues about God or gives reasons for believing in his existence. It takes him as the one great, original fact, the only reality. Its opening words are its great act of faith—' In the beginning God . . . ' ; he is the beginning and the end ; he is the One who ever was, who ever is, and who ever shall be.

We are not told of the struggle, by which Abraham came to believe in the one God. He lived in a land where many gods were worshipped, where there were great temples with great idols. There is a story in Jewish traditions of how Abraham, confident in his new-found faith in the one living, acting God, went one night into the local temple of the gods and smashed all the idols, except the greatest idol of all, in whose arms he placed the great hammer with which he had wrought this destruction. In the morning when the sacrilege was discovered, Abraham was called before the priests and

chiefs, and accused. In defence he pointed to the sole
surviving idol with the hammer in its arms, to which the
defenders of the faith replied in effect, ' Don't be foolish !
How could an idol do such a thing ? ' The consequent
shrug of Abraham's shoulders must have been most
expressive.

But Abraham's faith was not based on the reasoning of
the mind only or primarily. He had felt the nearness of
God, and heard him speak within his heart, persistently
and clearly. Finally, in response to that inner urging he
left the land of the idols and went out to seek a new
country, where he could be free to worship the one true
God and obey his will. His obedience made him the
father of the faithful—Jews, Christians, and Muslims all
acknowledge him as such.

Again and again, as we follow his pilgrimage of faith,
we read ' God appeared to Abraham,' or ' the Lord
spake unto Abraham '. Abraham did not have to seek
God : God came to him. And every fresh experience
strengthened his faith in the living God, who shows himself, who speaks, who commands, who blesses. One
great day he met another pioneer of faith, Melchizedek,
' priest of God most high '. How those two heroes of
faith must have rejoiced in each other, how encouraged
each must have been in the other's faith ! Melchizedek is
a mysterious figure, we know nothing of whence he came
or whither he went. He came, as it were, from outside,
sent by God, bringing bread and wine and the blessing
of God most high. No wonder faith and devotion see in
him the pre-figuring of another priest, coming from
outside, bringing bread and wine and blessing.

Moses at the burning bush is conscious of the divine
presence, and bares his feet in reverence and awe. Here
again it is God who speaks first and speaks a message as
shattering as that to Abraham. Moses is to return to
Egypt, to be under God the liberator of his chosen people.

A nation of slaves is to become the agent of his purpose and blessing, and God will seal his contract with them in the very place in which he now speaks. Moses is to announce him as the God of Abraham, who not only sees all that is happening to his enslaved people but has himself come to visit and liberate. Moses is still unsure of himself and wants to know by what name he shall announce God. The reply is simply, 'I AM hath sent me unto you.' I AM—nothing more than this, for there could be nothing more. I AM—the one eternal fact, the great reality from which everything derives, the source of all being, the ground of all existence, the only Being who can say, ' I AM ' in his own right. HE WHO IS. And a God who is unpredictable, who cannot be manipulated by men, who will measure up to no man's specifications— ' I AM THAT I AM,' or as the margin of the Revised Version says, ' I WILL BE THAT I WILL BE.' Man's only proper attitude in the presence of this reality is one of acceptance, obedience, worship.

The rest of the saga of Moses is dominated by this revelation. Moses takes everything to God—every reverse, every difficulty, every problem. The presence of God goes with him ; in the growing pains of faith Moses cries out, ' If thy presence go not with me, carry us not up hence.' God leads Moses into deeper knowledge of himself—' And the Lord spake unto Moses face to face, as a man speaketh unto his friend.'

Joshua, the soldier, hears God speak, ' As I was with Moses, so I will be with thee : I will not fail thee nor forsake thee. Be strong and of a good courage . . .' The child Samuel in the sanctuary at Shiloh hears God call ; as an old man he hears God's choice of David. Elijah is shown that God is not the God of the thunderstorm, the earthquake and the fire, but the God who speaks in the still small voice of the heart of those who stand before him in awe and worship. After Elijah comes a long line of prophets who dared to say, ' Thus saith the Lord,' regardless alike of the anger of kings and the opposition of the people, men who, when consulted, were prepared to wait until word came from the Lord. Isaiah worshipping in the temple sees the smoke of the morning sacrifice fade into the glory of heaven, with the burning holiness of God which makes him beat his breast in the thought of his own sinfulness. A weak, cowardly king comes secretly to Jeremiah in his dungeon to ask, ' Is there any word from the Lord ? ' It is no easy matter being the mouthpiece of the living God : on one occasion Jeremiah has to wait upon the Lord for ten days before the word comes ; at a later date it is only after seven days' vigil that the word comes to Ezekiel. We are sometimes tempted to think that the prophet's ' Thus saith the Lord ' was just a formula, the form in which he cast the message that he wanted to convey, that he thought appropriate to the moment, uttered as easily as the Anglican clergyman's ' In the Name of the Father and of the Son and of the Holy Ghost '. But it came in travail of spirit, in faithful waiting upon God until the heart knew that he had spoken. As we read the words of the prophets, in the light of later history, in the light of our Lord's supreme revelation, we cannot but be amazed at the sense of authenticity they convey. They are indeed more than human utterances, even though spoken through fallible men and voiced in human words.

The Jews are in truth the people of God, for God so constantly spoke to them. Always struggling for their existence, almost always under the domination of a great power, finally without a home-land, exiles in Babylon, without even a temple, nothing left to them but God. Even their ideas of God had to be broken and remade. They thought of him as the national god, limited to the frontiers of Israel. They complained, ' How can we sing the Lord's song in a strange land ? ' but defeated and deported, they find his presence there with them. They thought of him as their own possession, and they are told that Egypt and Assyria are alike his people. They think of him as the God of battles and according to human thinking he is repeatedly defeated. Gradually they learn that he is the God of all the earth, the Lord of all the nations. It is the Jews who ought to be able to tell us about God. Perhaps we shall never be able to tell the world convincingly about God, until the Jews have been won back to their divine mission. 'Now if their fall is the riches of the world, and their loss the riches of the Gentiles; how much more their fulness? . . . For if the casting away of them is the reconciling of the world, what shall the receiving of them be, but life from the dead?'

It is the Jews who can tell us about God, for they know what it is to have nothing to believe in except God. The vision of Zechariah 8 : 23 is still to be fulfilled : ' In those days it shall come to pass, that ten men (the number necessary before a synagogue can be formed) shall take hold out of all the languages of the nations, even shall take hold of the skirt of him that is a Jew, saying, We will go with you ; for we have heard that God is with you.'

Jews and Christians, however, are not the only people who believe in a God who reveals himself. Muslims do also. For, 2,500 years after Abraham, another Semite came to a similar faith in God and a rejection of idols— Mohammed in Arabia. Just about the time that Augustine of Canterbury was preaching the Gospel in Kent, Mohammed underwent a series of spiritual experiences which he interpreted as direct revelations from the God of Abraham. Like Abraham he was used to long journeys across the sandy deserts and quiet nights under the stars. Living among Jews and Christians he expected some interest from them in his revelations, but was disappointed.

In the early days of his preaching he directed his followers to pray towards Jerusalem, but when opposition from Christians and Jews increased he bade them turn towards Mecca.

There was no Melchizedek to encourage and confirm Mohammed's faith. What a difference there might have been in religious history had there been someone to be the friend to him that Melchizedek had been to Abraham, who would have said to him, ' Yes, it is the God of Abraham who has revealed himself to you. Let me tell you of our experience of him, and together let us see his will for you and for the people of Arabia.' If there had been an early friend who could have introduced him to the Gospels and the revelation of God in Christ, instead of the garbled accounts he had heard, Mohammed could well have been the greatest Christian missionary since S. Paul.

The God who spoke to the fathers and the prophets in time past still speaks directly to men today. About fifty years ago a Buddhist hermit in Burma, U Tha Dun, without any previous contact with Christian missionaries, came to believe in the existence of the Eternal God and went about Lower Burma preaching his newly found faith. One day he went to reprove a woman disciple of his, who had become a Christian, and he arrived at her village at the time that a big rural conference was being held by the Christians of the neighbourhood. There he listened to Christian preaching about the revelation of the eternal God in Jesus Christ, and came to believe in Christ as Lord and Saviour. The remaining years of his life he spent in preaching Christ—in market-places, on steamers and trains, anywhere where men would listen.

The God of the Bible is alive and active, a God who is always near yet wholly other, a curious God who wants to know what is going on, an interfering God who will have his way because he knows it is for man's ultimate good and happiness, who has his appropriate counter-move for every rebellion of men, who speaks through world happenings and in the hearts of men, so that they may be under no misapprehension as to what he is trying to do.

But the man who does not believe in God may well say, ' You have told me what your faith is, and I can see that it is a good faith, if it is true. But I don't want to live in a fool's paradise, so give me reasons for believing what you do.'

Here we must be honest, and admit quite frankly that there is no proof or argument which in itself will convince the non-believer. There are, however, certain clues which are worth following. Ever since men began to think, they have been wondering how the universe came into being. The materialist view is that matter and space have always existed and that matter, behaving in fixed ways, has happened by a fluke or accident to produce creatures like ourselves who are able to think. By chance something hit the sun and produced the planets, by further chance something produced the right conditions of life on one of these planets, and then by a long series of chances living creatures developed into men. Still increasing chance produced Abraham, Zoroaster, the Buddha, Isaiah, Jesus, Paul, you and me. Mathematicians will tell you what astronomical odds there are against such a series of happenings. On the other hand, there is the religious view, which says that the universe came into being through the action of a Personal Creator, who created men like himself and planned that they should live in a conscious relationship with himself as his children. Each man has to decide which view seems more reasonable.

A second clue may be found in the consideration of the order and purpose of the universe. When you examine what goes on in the world of nature you find that everything works according to law. The planets go round the sun, night and day unceasingly alternate, the seasons come round with unfailing regularity, seeds germinate, grow and produce their harvest year after year. There is a remarkable regularity and order. The various processes of nature seem to dovetail into one another in a co-ordinated scheme. The whole universe speaks of order and purpose. Is it not reasonable to suppose that behind this unfailing order there is a Mind at work—the Mind of the Maker?

Still a third clue may be discovered from the fact that wherever you go in the world you find people with some kind of standard of decent behaviour. Everywhere people feel that it is wrong to break a promise, to run away in danger or to double-cross your neighbour. Whenever two people quarrel, each tries to show that the other is wrong, as if there were some independent standard of behaviour. From where does this sense of right and wrong come? Some people say that the moral law is just our herd instinct or that it is something impressed upon us by parents and teachers. But how did it originate? It looks as if there were some controlling power outside myself, which is always urging me to do right and makes me feel responsible when I do wrong.

This argument from the existence of the moral law in man should be of interest to the Buddhist for he has great reverence for what he calls the *Dhamma*, or Law, which means more to him than just the teaching of the Buddha. It is the order of law in the universe, which combines both reason and morality. The Buddhist thinks of this law as eternal and uncreated, something which Buddhas and good men discover. Christians in Ceylon are discussing this point with Buddhists suggesting that you must either think of *Dhamma* as mind and therefore personal, or you must think of a mind and person, who is the source and sustainer of *Dhamma*.

The reason of the mind, therefore, urges us to belief in God; experience in life tests and confirms our faith.

There is something further, less tangible, less easy to put into words. This is our own direct experience of God in prayer and worship. There are times when prayer is difficult, when our hearts are cold and dry, when God seems far away, when prayer is an effort and worship a duty. There are other times when we know ourselves to be in the presence of the living God, when the mind almost ceases to think, when there is no need of words, because he has come to us, and our hearts are at peace. When we make a practice of the presence of God—not a hurried entrance and the recital of a few prayers or the rapid mention of the names of people for whom we know we ought to pray—but a quiet, reverent, loving waiting upon him, a lifting of the heart to him in praise and thanksgiving, a communion of spirit with Spirit, of heart with Heart, when time seems to stand still because we are in eternity, then something of the divine presence clings to us as we return to our everyday life. As we lift up our faces to the glory of God, we shall reflect its light, and men will see and know that we have been with God.

Somehow we have to present God so that he becomes real to others, to Hindus or modern agnostics who believe that he is unknowable, to many Buddhists or Communists who do not even believe in his existence. The effective way is the way of the Bible—making God the great reality of our own lives. ' God is the only reality,' says S. Augustine of Hippo, ' and we are only real in so far as we are in his order and he in us.' In all our thinking the whole emphasis must be on God—his purpose, his initiative, his will. Apart from him we should never have come into existence. He keeps us moment by moment, our relationship to him is our only hope of eternity. He must be the very centre of our being. When other people come to see that God is the great reality in our lives, there is some hope that they will examine more closely the words in which we try to speak of him.

PRAYERS

God is what thought cannot better ;
God is whom thought cannot reach ;
God no thinking can even conceive.
Without God, men can have no being,
   no reason, no knowledge, no good desire, naught.
Thou, O God, art what thou art,
   transcending all.

E. Milner-White

Almighty God,
   Give us wisdom to perceive thee,
   intelligence to understand thee,
   diligence to seek thee,
   patience to wait for thee,
   eyes to behold thee,
   a heart to meditate upon thee,
   and a life to proclaim thee.

S. Benedict (480–543)

God be in my head, and in my understanding ;
God be in mine eyes, and in my looking ;
God be in my mouth, and in my speaking ;
God be in my heart, and in my thinking ;
God be at mine end, and at my departing.

Sarum Primer, 1558

To God,
   Whom no eye hath seen,
Nor ear hath heard,
Yet who speaks to the heart
   of all that love him :
To him be praise and glory for ever and ever.

London Service Book

Suggestions for meditation and discussion after chapters I - VI are included at the end of the book on page 87.

CHAPTER II

GOD WAS IN CHRIST

In the Old Testament God spoke to men, in Christ God came to men : more even than that, in Christ God became man, something far more telling and unbelievably wonderful: that the Creator should become a creature, the Eternal express himself in time. God became man ! Muslims so emphasise the majesty and transcendence of God that they cannot conceive him associating himself in such a way with man. No wonder that many Christians feel they must kneel at the very mention—' Who for us men, and our salvation came down from heaven. And was incarnate by the Holy Ghost of the Virgin Mary, And was made man.'

God from the beginning has been speaking to men divine words, now at last he speaks the Word from within his own being. Men have to express themselves through words, they can only convey to one another what is in their inmost heart and mind through speech. God expresses his heart in Jesus Christ, who is his Eternal Word. The One who has ever been with God now comes forth to men. ' No man hath seen God at any time ; the only begotten Son, which is in the bosom of the Father, he hath declared him.' ' The Word was with God, and the Word was God. . . . And the Word was made flesh, and dwelt among us.'

Now men may know what God is like, for one who has been with him from all eternity has shown us in terms of a human life. God has become one of us. The problem of communication is solved : God puts himself in our position and we may understand. Like Son, like

Father. ' He that hath seen me hath seen the Father.' Jesus is ' the image of the invisible God,' ' the express image of his person ' and ' the brightness of his glory '. Whenever we want to know anything about God we look at Jesus Christ. How does God behave towards the sinner ? What is his attitude to the sick, the blind, the demented ? Look at Jesus Christ and know. We must test all our thinking about God by Jesus Christ. ' It was said by them of old time . . . but I say unto you '— this is true of men's ideas about God as well as of ethical standards. Jesus Christ is the visible expression of God.

The fact that God became a ' human ' God is startling enough ; the way in which he did it is equally startling. He did not burst into human life in a blinding theophany, as we would have expected. He was born as a helpless baby in a stable. Somehow he had to prove that although he dwelt in light unapproachable, he *was* approachable, that he was not only loving but lovable. There is nothing more helpless and dependent than a new-born baby. The baby in the manger at Bethlehem was God. If ever there was a case of ' my thoughts are not your thoughts ', Bethlehem was such. God completely disarmed our fear by putting himself into our hands as a baby, as if to say, ' Here I am, do with me what you will.'

There is a divine helplessness and defencelessness in this renunciation of power in which God's Son abandoned his glory and entered the world as a slave. He came not to be waited upon, but to wait upon others, and to give his life that men might no longer be the slaves of self or of the devil but God's freed men. In Christ God deliber- ately reduced himself to our level, to the point where all of us have to start : ' He emptied himself,' says S. Paul ; he took the nature which we share, and showed through it the life and character of God. Not only did he reveal God to us through it, but he showed us how God meant

men to be and live. Beginning in exactly the same way
as we have to, he showed how men with that handicap
could live and die and rise again by the power of God.
His favourite expression for himself was ' Son of Man ',
meaning representative man, man as he was in the
original purposes of God, man as he was always meant to
be. He showed in truth that man could be the child of
God.

All through his incarnate life Jesus accepted this
limitation and self-emptying. The religious leaders
repeatedly demanded a sign from heaven : his own
disciples protested ' this shall never happen unto thee ' ;
the devil, conscious of crisis in his own kingdom, was
always at hand to tempt him to use his power. Our
modern phrase ' Be yourself ! ' well expresses the subtlety
of the devil's approach, which continued to the final
temptation, ' Come down from the cross, and we will
believe.' Even then the devil was not finished ; his last
desperate effort was the most deadly of all—' God has
forsaken you,' ' God is no longer in Christ reconciling the
world unto himself.'

At Calvary Christ showed God to be as humble and
defenceless as at Bethlehem. It was essential for men to
know that God loved them to the uttermost, that there
was nothing which men could do to God which would
lessen his love or limit his forgiveness. So when men
nailed God-become-man to a cross, all that burst from
his lips was the prayer, ' Father, forgive them ; for they
know not what they do.' In that prayer there was not
only the highest expression of God's love, but also the
unquenchable hope that, when men had seen God bear
the last possible humiliation, they would begin to know
what they were doing and what God had been doing from
Bethlehem to Calvary.

Yet with all this defencelessness Jesus was fully conscious of who he was. He claimed that the words he

spoke were words he heard the Father speaking, the
things he did were the things God was always doing.
When he healed the sick, touched the leper and blessed
the children, he was expressing in human action the compassion and love of God. Some of the things he said
about himself stretched the faith of his followers to the
utmost limit, as they still stretch our faith : I am the
Truth ; I am the Life ; I am the Way ; I am the Door ;
I am the Light of the World ; I am the Resurrection and
the Life ; I am the Bread of Life ; Before Abraham was
I AM ; I and the Father are one. What can we think of
a person who makes these claims about himself ? Many
of those who heard him just could not accept these
claims. The religious leaders accused him of blasphemy,
saying most truly that he made himself the equal of God.
At one time his own family wanted to restrain him from
preaching, ' For,' they said, ' he is beside himself ' ; in
other words they feared he was mad. There can only be
two logical opinions about Jesus Christ—either he was
what he said he was, or he was a deluded lunatic. Many
people are prepared to accept Jesus as the greatest of all
religious teachers, to accept his teaching about God and
the Kingdom, even to try and live according to the
standards which he taught, but are not willing to accept
him as God. But you cannot pick and choose what you
will accept and what you will reject. It is all or nothing.
If he was mistaken about his relationship to God, he was
a dangerous deceiver and the Jews were right to crucify
him. But if he was right, the only thing is to accept him
as Lord and God.

From the beginning of his ministry people were puzzled
by him : ' What is this ? a new teaching ! with authority
he commandeth even the unclean spirits and they obey
him.' ' Whence hath this man these things ? ' Even
when rejecting his claims the Jews felt compelled to add
' as for this man, we know not whence he is.' The Roman

Governor at his trial seemed for a moment to get a glimpse of something out of the ordinary and asks his prisoner, ' Whence art thou ? ' Pilate's wife was even more puzzled.

It is revealing to trace the development of the disciples' thought about him. First of all they were attracted by him as a teacher, who spoke with an authentic note about God, unlike the religious teachers of the day who were always quoting this or that rabbi. His teaching about himself as the bread of life had strained the faith of many, but Peter and his companions knew that there was no one else to whom they could go, for ' thou hast the words of eternal life '. Gradually they came to accept him as the Christ, the Messiah, the Hope of Israel. They came to this faith not so much by logical reasoning, but by an intuition which Jesus himself said came from God. This leap of faith was confirmed in the Transfiguration, when the three most intimate of his disciples saw the eternal glory. Yet even now full understanding had not dawned on them, though the incident said to them, ' This is my beloved Son, in whom I am well pleased ; obey him.' Their growing expectations, however, were soon shattered by his arrest and death. ' We hoped that it was he who should have redeemed Israel,' said the two friends sadly to the stranger who walked with them on the road to Emmaus. Then came the climax of triumph and faith. Thomas's ' My Lord and my God ' shows the last doubt removed ; as they returned from the Mount of Olives, ' they worshipped him and returned to Jerusalem with great joy.' Jesus was *Lord*.

S. Paul who found it more difficult than any other of the early disciples to accept the idea of a crucified Christ, later came to see that the cross was the crowning glory of God's self-disclosure. All down the centuries since Calvary men have tried to interpret what happened there. Sometimes they have thought of a righteous and angry God being propitiated by the sacrifice of the sinless Christ. S. Paul will have none of this. ' God was in Christ reconciling the world unto himself.' There was no difference in heart or will or being between Christ and God : ' God was in Christ,' ' God commendeth his own love toward us, in that, while we were yet sinners, Christ died for us.'

Men by their sins had gone away from God and had not been able to find their way back. So God came in Christ to go out and find the lost. Men by their sins had erected a barrier between themselves and God, which they were unable to break down or cross over. The only thing that could break through the barrier was perfect holiness, and men were incapable of this. So Christ came from God to break down the barrier. Men had fallen under the domination of evil ; Christ came to defeat the devil and set the prisoners free.

In the estrangement of God and man caused by man's sin, God came in Christ to bring about a reconciliation. God took the first step, held out the hand of friendship, made friends with men. In the paralytic at Capernaum Christ saw every man's need of forgiveness, and before a word of penitence had been uttered spoke the words of gospel ' Thy sins be forgiven thee ' ; and to prove the inner reality of forgiveness he worked the external miracle of healing. Yet even this was not proof enough, for there were worse sins than those that paralysed the man of Capernaum. Men needed to be shown that there was nothing they could do to God which could not be included in God's forgiveness. So when men crucified God-in-Christ, the first words that came to his lips were, ' Father, forgive '.

That God should allow men to execute him is well nigh unbelievable. Muslims, who only accept Jesus as a prophet, cannot believe that God would so let down one of his prophets as to allow him to be crucified.

' They did not kill him,' says the Qur'an, ' they did not crucify him, but one was made to resemble him.' So many Muslims believe that God turned the tables on Judas by allowing the traitor to be crucified in place of the master whom he had betrayed. Could anything be farther from the faith of S. Paul that ' God was in Christ reconciling the world unto himself ' ?

In his human life God-in-Christ plumbed the deepest depths of human experience. He experienced poverty, obscurity, homelessness, the misunderstanding of friends, the relentless opposition of people who claimed to be the people of God and yet plotted to get rid of him by murder, the technique of the devil. He saw men's sufferings and carried them on his heart. He saw that they were spiritually leaderless, lost as sheep without a shepherd, and his heart was filled with sadness and compassion for them. He saw their misunderstanding of God, how they attributed to his Father the sufferings which were never part of his will and, even when coming through sin or mysterious accident, were all opportunities for God's glory and love to be revealed.

In only one thing was he different from men—sharing our infirmities and tempted in all things even as we are, he was without sin. How can he then understand the hopelessness and despair of men who sin, who long to get free from the devil's power and the fallen weakness of their own nature ? It is true that Jesus was without sin, yet is it not true that the man who really knows the power of evil is not the man who succumbs to temptation so easily and so repeatedly, nor he who yields after a struggle, but he who resists to the very end, who has come through not only the crude temptations of the flesh and the world, but the subtle temptations of the spirit which the devil brings against those who threaten his kingdom ?

Think of some of Christ's temptations in the wilderness ;

he was tempted to use his power for his own benefit, to display his power in some spectacular way to compel men's belief, to compromise with devil and the world in order to win men's loyalty. But he knew that none of these things would change men's hearts. God's love must be shown to the uttermost and that involved from the start the possibility of rejection, suffering, and even death. Right to the end the devil continued his efforts to defeat Christ and to deflect him from the Father's purpose. In Gethsemane he was tempted to doubt that the cross was God's will, God's chosen way of saving the world ; at Calvary his enemies hurled at him the cry, ' Come down from the cross and we will believe,' and challenged his faith, ' He trusted in God ; let God deliver him now if he desireth him.' Then finally the most subtle temptation of all ' God has forsaken you ! God has forsaken you ! ' which only served to recall to his mind a psalm on which he must have often meditated. Psalm 22, which opens with the words, ' My God, my God, why hast thou forsaken me ', was written by a man in great trouble and danger, racked by a wasting illness and at the mercy of his enemies. It so obviously fitted the situation in which our Lord found himself, in excruciating pain, forsaken by most of his friends, surrounded by snarling enemies, seemingly forsaken by God. All through his life he had been able to say, ' I am not alone, because the Father is with me,' but now even God seems hidden.

In the Church of S. John, Waterloo Road, the church restored during the Festival of Britain in 1953, there is behind the altar a painting by Hans Feibusch of the crucifixion, in which small figures of angels and devils are flying round the crucified Christ. The effect is one of struggle and crisis, arousing in the mind of those who stand long enough to enter into the spirit of the artist, the sense of spiritual forces engaged in a crucial and final struggle as if everything depended on its outcome.

We can reverently imagine our Lord following the words of the psalm, with its great opening cry to God and its alternating rhythm of desolation and faith, until at length it rises to the triumphant assurance of faith ' All the ends of the earth shall remember and turn unto the Lord : and all the kindreds of the nations shall worship before thee. For the kingdom is the Lord's : and he is the ruler over the nations.' What a faith for a man dying on a cross ! What a plumbing of the lowest depths of man's desolation by God-become-man !

A few minutes later that great cry is followed by a still greater cry, ' It is finished ! ' A cry of triumph that God's will has been done completely and utterly, God-in-Christ has reconciled the world unto himself, a new and living way has been opened into the presence of God, and through it grateful, forgiven and believing men may find their way back to the Father's arms. In the parable of the son who came home, Jesus told us that while he was yet a great way off his father saw him and was moved with compassion, and ran and fell on his neck and kissed him. In Christ, God came to meet sinful man, took him in his arms and kissed him.

The New Testament tells us that it was by his cross and passion that Christ saved us from our sins. Sin keeps us away from God ; where there is no sin there is no separation between man and God. Jesus was one in heart and will with God ; he hated sin as God did, because he saw how it grieved God, how it damaged men and kept them from God. At the moment when Jesus died upon the cross, there was for the first time in human history a man completely obedient to the will of God, even unto death. And therefore the love and power of God could flow into him without interruption. Jesus is God and man : on the Godward side he is one with God, on the manward side he is united with man. The love and power of God can flow through him into all men who join themselves to him in faith and commitment. In that love and power, man not only knows that God loves him and that God has forgiven him, but he can receive Christ's life, the life that has come unscathed and victorious through evil and death. So he receives not only new status and forgiveness, but a transfusion of life that enables him to live the life of a child of God.

What happened at Calvary was a turning point in the history of mankind. The writer of the first gospel, with the insight of an artist and prophet, describes a group of events connected with the death of Christ : darkness covers the land, the veil of the temple separating the worshippers from the Holy of Holies is torn in two, the earth is shaken and rocks are rent, and the bodies of dead saints come out of their graves.

Paul Tillich in one of his sermons interprets these signs as showing :

. . . that the event at Golgotha is one which concerns the universe, including all nature and all history. . . .

The sun veiled its face because of the depth of evil and shame which it saw under the Cross. But the sun also veiled its face because its power over the world had ceased once and forever in those hours of darkness. The great shining and burning god of everything that lives on the earth, the sun who was praised and feared and adored by innumerable beings during thousands and thousands of years, had been deprived of its divine power when *one* human being in ultimate agony maintained his unity with that which is greater than the sun. . . .

. . . The temple tore its gown as the mourners did because He, to whom the temple belonged more than to anyone else, was thrown out and killed by the servants of the temple. But the temple—and with it, all temples on earth—also complained of its own destiny. The curtain which made the temple a holy place, separated from other places, lost its separating

power.   He who was expelled as blaspheming the
temple, had cleft the curtain and opened the temple
for everybody, for every moment. . . .   After this
moment temples and churches can only mean places
of concentration on the holy which is the ground and
the meaning of every place.   And like the temple, the
earth was judged at Golgotha.   Trembling and shaking
the earth participated in the agony of the man on the
Cross and in the despair of all those who had seen in
Him the beginning of the new eon.   Trembling and
shaking the earth proved that it is not the motherly
ground on which we can safely build our houses and
cities, our cultures and religious systems.   Trembling
and shaking the earth pointed to another ground on
which the earth itself rests : the self-surrendering love
on which all earthly powers and values concentrate
their hostility and which they cannot conquer. . . .

And the earth not only ceases to be the solid ground
of life ; she also ceases to be the lasting cave of death.
. . . No longer is the universe subjected to the law of
death out of birth.   It is subjected to a higher law, to
the law of life out of death by the death of Him who
represented eternal life.   The tombs were opened and
bodies were raised when one man in whom God was
present without limit committed His spirit into His
Father's hands.   Since this moment the universe is no
longer what it was ; nature has received another
meaning ; history is transformed and you and I are
no more, and should not be any more, what we were
before. [1]

The faith of the New Testament is simple and clear :
Jesus Christ is not just the best of men ; nor the greatest
of teachers ; he is not a holy man taken up into the
Godhead when the Spirit of God descended upon him ;
Jesus Christ is Lord and God. If we accept this, then
all our thinking and living must be governed by this

[1] Paul Tillich, *The New Being* (S.C.M. Press)

central fact ; that conviction must possess both mind and heart. His words will then come to us with the authority of God's words. His will become the strongest desire, the foundation aim of our lives. If Jesus Christ is God, then I must love him with all my heart, with all my mind, with all my soul and with all my strength.

In this faith, Christ is the gospel, the good news we take to the world. He is God's ultimate Word to men, he is Truth, he is Life, he is Love, he is Forgiveness, he is Salvation and Power. ' Woe is unto me, if I preach not the Gospel,' for if I preach not the Gospel it means that I do not really believe it, that I have never experienced it.

To us Christians this action of God in Christ seems such obviously good news that we see little need to amplify it. But the Muslim, like the Jew, rejects the thought of God becoming man. To him God is so full of majesty and omnipotence that he cannot conceive him lowering himself to associate with man in the incarnation. There are a number of misconceptions among Muslims of what Christians believe : one is that Christians believe in three Gods. This may be due to the undisciplined way in which many Christians express their faith in the Holy Trinity. We start as firmly as Jews and Muslims from the belief in one God ; the experience of the Apostles and of succeeding generations of disciples has led us to believe that within the Being of the one God there are eternal relationships, corresponding to God's revelation of himself as Creator, as Incarnate Lord, as indwelling Spirit. Let us be more God-centred in our language, as the title of this chapter insists, God was in Christ. In our conversations with Jews and Muslims, let us always begin with God—God was in Christ, Christ is God with men, the Holy Spirit is God in men—God, God, God, the one and only God. But let us not forget that there are some great misunderstandings among Muslims, many of whom think that we Christians believe in God the Father, the Virgin Mary, and the Son who was born of a union between them similar to the intercourse of gods and women in Greek and pagan myths, an idea as abhorrent to Christians as to Muslims.

Muslims believe as firmly as Christians do, in God's revelation to men. The Qur'an says, ' If the sea were ink for the words of my Lord, the sea would surely be exhausted before the words of my Lord were exhausted.' When we talk with Muslims we might well use S. John's title, ' The Word ', for Jesus ; it is one which Muslims would understand. The first requisite is that Muslims shall really understand what we are saying to them. They may still reject it, but we owe it to them to make sure that they know what they are rejecting.

Having disposed of misunderstandings, we can then go on to talk together of the sovereignty of God and his freedom to do as he wills. Do not our Muslim friends limit the sovereignty of God, if they insist that God could not possibly have become man ? Can we creatures of God tell our Creator what he may do and what he may not do ? Similarly with the Crucifixion, may we men dictate to God how he is to save us ? Humanly speaking, it was unforgivable for men to crucify God, yet the Christian faith is that this is just what men did to God, and God let them do it, and God forgave. The very idea of God implies sovereignty : God in Christ proclaims that sovereignty is not sufficient as a description of his character ; love is an equally eternal characteristic of his nature. We must hold on to both. Love is seen supremely in the Crucifixion ; so also is sovereignty, for that is the way that God himself chose, against all the expectations and logic of men. Sovereignty is seen supremely in the Resurrection, and love is shown to be triumphant.

PRAYERS

Lord, let me kneel before thy miracle,
   —an infant in a stable
   on a human mother's breast,
from all eternity thine only begotten Son,
   thy Word from before beginning,
God of God, Light of Light, Very God of Very God,
   of his own choice, of thine own purpose,
   made mortal man. . . .
O Christ, let me kneel before the wonder of thy Glory
   thus made manifest to all flesh ; . . .

E. Milner-White

All glory, praise and thanks be to thee, Eternal God,
that out of the darkness which enfolds thee has
appeared a light, and out of the silence in which
thou dwellest has sounded a voice, so that thou art
no longer unknown to us thy creatures. The face of
Jesus is thy light, and the Cross of Jesus is thy voice.
Grant that we may so meditate upon his life, and so
enter into the fellowship of his sacrifice, that we may
know thee as thou truly art, holy and compassionate,
righteous and loving unto sinners, and knowing thee
in thy Son, may give thee an offering which thou
desirest, even ourselves to be thy servants.
Through the same Jesus Christ, our Saviour.

W. R. Matthews

Blessed be thy name, O Jesu,
   Son of the most high God ;
Blessed be the sorrow thou sufferedst
   When thy holy hands and feet were nailed
     To the tree ;
   And blessed thy love when,
     The fulness of pain accomplished,
Thou didst give thy soul into the hands
   Of the Father ;

So by thy Cross and precious Blood
Redeeming all the world,
All longing souls departed
And the numberless unborn ;
Who now livest and reignest in the glory
Of the eternal Trinity
For ever and ever.

E. Milner-White

CHAPTER III

THE NEW ORDER IN CHRIST

It is a tremendous act of faith to accept Jesus Christ as Lord, so great that S. Paul says it can only be done in the Holy Spirit. To him the proof that Jesus is Lord lay in the resurrection : he ' was declared to be the Son of God with power, according to the spirit of holiness, by the resurrection of the dead.' It was his experience of the risen Christ on the Damascus road which led him to the words of surrender, ' Lord, what wilt thou have me to do ? '

The cross and resurrection are at the heart of his preaching, for ' if Christ hath not been raised from the dead, then is our preaching vain, your faith also is vain . . . ye are yet in your sins.' So Paul is careful to give the evidence for the resurrection. In 1 Cor. 15 : 4–8, he lists the witnesses, of whom the majority were still alive at the time when he was writing, some twenty-five years later. Yet he devotes barely fifty words to the eye witnesses, and often speaks in a way that makes witnesses almost unnecessary. When talking about the power of God Paul always speaks of it as shown in the resurrection ; his aim is to know the power of Christ's resurrection and the fellowship of his sufferings. Paul always starts from the resurrection ; he does not work towards it, but argues from it. The fact of the resurrection is so great and his own experience of it so deep, that he needs no more convincing witness.

To most Christians the first and most obvious good news in the resurrection of Jesus is the hope that death is not the end, that there is life after death, that one day

we shall be re-united with our loved ones who have died.
Let us give full value to this. It was pre-figured in our
Lord's miracles of resurrection, the raising of the daughter
of Jairus, of the widow's son at Nain, and of Lazarus of
Bethany. These between them cover the range of human
life and all the stages of death. The little girl of twelve
with all the promise of life before her, the young man in
all his powers of early manhood, the mature man support-
ing the home at Bethany, all three taken by death hear
the voice of the Lord and return to life in the world.
The first case is a deathbed in which the soul has barely
left the body ; the second is a funeral, with the corpse
stiffened in death ; in the third the body has already
begun to decay in the grave. All three spirits are within
call of the Lord's voice, all three bodies in varying stages
of dissolution are within his re-creating power. Jesus
is seen to be Lord of death and Lord of life ; he has made
good in these three instances his eternal claim, ' I am
the resurrection, and the life : he that believeth on me,
though he die, yet shall he live.' The hour indeed has
come, ' when the dead shall hear the voice of the Son of
God ; and they that hear shall live.'
By his miracles of healing the Lord has shown us that
God is on the side of health and strength, by his miracles
of resurrection the Lord has shown us that God is on the
side of life. Yet little ones still die before they have had
a real chance of life, young men are cut off in their prime,
people of maturity and wisdom die just when they have
learnt some of the secrets of how God means us to live.
There is still a mystery of suffering and death which we
cannot fully understand. Doubtless many deaths are
due to mistaken ways of living of which we are not yet
conscious, the exact causes and cures of which scientists
and doctors have not so far been able to discover. The
three resurrection miracles are sufficient to show us that
those who die are still within reach of our Lord's voice

and power. ' For whether we live, we live unto the
Lord ; or whether we die, we die unto the Lord:
whether we live therefore, or die, we are the Lord's.
For to this end Christ died, and lived again, that he
might be Lord of both the dead and the living.' Christ's
own resurrection confirms the lordship of life and death
shown in the earlier examples. Like Paul we start and
end with Christ : Christ rose from the dead, therefore
resurrection is not only possible, it is the foundation of
the true and eternal world.

Christ died, ' that through death he might bring to
nought him that had the power of death, that is, the devil ;
and might deliver all them who through fear of death
were all their lifetime subject to bondage.' Everywhere
men fear death, and try to keep the thought of their own
death from their minds. Even with our faith in Christ
as the conqueror of death, the prospect of death is a
solemn and awe-inspiring thought. A character in a
modern novel voices both the fear of death and the love
of life :

And, when the years have all passed, then will gape
the uncomfortable and unpredictable dark void of
death, and into this I shall at last fall headlong, down
and down and down, and the prospect of that fall,
that uprooting, that rending apart of body and spirit,
that taking off into so blank an unknown, drowns me
in mortal fear and mortal grief. After all, life, for all
its agonies of despair and loss and guilt, is exciting and
beautiful, amusing and artful and endearing, full of
liking and of love, at times a poem and a high adventure,
at times noble and at times very gay ; and whatever
(if anything) is to come after it, we shall not have this
life again.[1]

Death has become an enemy through sin, and S. Paul

---

[1] Rose Macaulay, *The Towers of Trebizond* (Collins)

says that it will be the last enemy to be destroyed. Without God in Christ death is the irreparable disaster. As Bishop Stephen Neill says :

> There is no anguish of anticipation or of fear in the death of the beasts ; there should be none in the death of a man. The distortion of values which sin has brought about has made this life seem immensely precious, and the loss of it the one final and irreparable disaster. Alienation from God has made it hard to believe that to fall asleep here is no more than to awaken elsewhere. The sense of guilt and unpaid debts arouses fears of strict accounting and retribution. If the presence of God is withdrawn, to die is to step out into an unknown and horrifying abyss.[1]

With the weakening of Christian faith in the west, the accepted idea seems to be that at all costs doctors and hospitals should keep the spark of human life alive even if the mental powers are almost gone and the body hardly functioning. Without faith in a future life people seem to think that the supreme value lies in hanging on in this life, however paralysed or ineffective it may be. It is only when we have a deep faith in resurrection that we can say with S. Paul, ' To depart and be with Christ . . . is very far better.' We can learn a lesson here from the good Buddhist who believes that it is a mistake to cling to anything, including human life itself. This teaching is, of course, quite clear in the New Testament where Our Lord teaches us that he who puts the saving of his life as the highest value will lose the deepest spiritual life, the only life which is eternal.

In a largely non-Christian country a Christian death-bed or a Christian funeral affords very telling witness of the gospel of the resurrection. There is inevitably the grief of separation, but it is not a sorrow without hope.

[1] From an unpublished MS. by Bishop Stephen Neill

The dominant note is quiet trust in God, the assurance that our Lord's victory extends over the kingdom of the dead as well as over this world, and the thought that to the man who trusts in Christ death is no more than falling asleep in this world and waking up in the next.

Those who have worked in the world mission of the Church know much of the terror and despair of death in non-Christian countries, and of the fear of the spirits of the dead. In the Kachin Hills in the north of Burma, a bamboo ladder is often let down into the grave and the spirit priest addresses the dead man by name, bidding his spirit leave the body, climb the ladder and go away from the village, down the hill, crossing the stream where a thread of cotton has been tied across as a bridge, and away to the country of the dead, where he is to stay and return no more to haunt his family and village.

The writer remembers very vividly an incident in his early years in Burma, where after the funeral of a Christian student, he was approached by a Buddhist member of staff and a group of Buddhist students and asked to place a notice of dismissal on the grave, ' Maung Ba Than, take notice that your name has today been struck off the register of the school, so return no more.'

Contrast this fear of the dead with the words of commendation often spoken at a Christian deathbed :

Go forth upon thy journey from this world,
O Christian soul,
    In the name of God the Father Almighty who created thee.
    In the name of Jesus Christ who suffered for thee.
    In the name of the Holy Ghost who strengtheneth thee.
    In communion with the blessed Saints, and aided by Angels and Archangels, and all the armies of the heavenly host.

May thy portion this day be in peace, and thy dwelling in the heavenly Jerusalem.[1]

In the resurrection the body of Jesus was transformed and transfigured. His earthly life, his passion and death are incorporated into it, as the marks of the five wounds show, but it is a glorified body raised above all the limitations of time and space. When the Word took flesh, it was not only for the thirty-three years of his incarnate life, but for eternity. When he entered into eternal glory he did not discard his humanity but took it with him—transformed and transfigured, but for ever recognizable as the body which was offered in love on the cross. The resurrection, therefore, is not just the proof of survival after death, it is the pledge that the whole of our nature shall be redeemed, body as well as mind and spirit, transformed and transfigured but recognizably the heir of our corporal body.

In the Risen Christ as he showed himself to his friends during the great forty days between his resurrection and ascension, we see man as he will be when, through Christ, he comes to the perfection which God wills for him. ' For six weeks of springtime nineteen centuries ago the perfected Man was seen and loved on the same earth that the unfallen Adam, the germinal Man, had walked millions of years before, and that we live in now. At will he showed himself, at will he was unseen. He consorted with his friends, went for walks, and shared a supper, and picnicked by the lake. Nothing could have been homelier, nothing more natural. For it was natural ; that is the point. And his sole Resurrection from the un-numbered myriads of the dead is the pledge and proof that the road to Man's natural perfection once more lies open to all the sons of men.' [2]

[1] From *The Book of Common Prayer with the Additions and Deviations Proposed in 1928* (Oxford University Press)

[2] A Religious of C.S.M.V., *As in Adam* (Mowbray)

The Risen Christ is a life-giving spirit. Paul spoke of him as the second Adam, the head of the new humanity, and all men may participate in his reign of life, if they will. This new life is not reserved until after death, but is available now. It was Paul's participation in the new life which was to him the most convincing evidence of Christ's resurrection, and the resurrection was to him the proof that Jesus is Lord and God.

' If any man is in Christ,' says S. Paul, ' he is a new creature : the old things are passed away ; behold, they are become new.' In talking with Nicodemus Jesus said that unless a man were born again, he could not see, let alone enter, the Kingdom of God, and he went on to say that the second birth was from above, the gift of God. You cannot enter the Kingdom without the new birth, but you are given it freely by God. Nicodemus saw the difficulty of it from the human angle : how can a man be born again when he is old ? A man at any stage of his life is the product of all his past, how can he suddenly change ? It is as difficult as to return to his mother's womb. As a man grows older he gets settled in his habits, his character becomes clearly delineated and is recognized by his friends. How can he change ? The answer is that when he commits himself to Christ, he is given a new birth. Perhaps what happens is easier to understand if we think of it as Christ being born in each believer. This new birth is only a beginning ; it does not mean that we become holy over-night as if by a stroke of magic. Christ is born in us, we must allow him to grow up in us, to live in us. The old nature will still be there, but there will be a new power at work within it, though it will take time before we are fully redeemed. There will be a persistent struggle between Christ in us and the old nature. There will be tension between my longing after the full stature of Christ in me and the pull-back of the old life, between the holiness of Christ in me and my existence in unredeemed human nature. But a new process of renewal and transformation has started, begun in the risen power of Christ.

The very possibility of this new birth is good news to fallen, struggling men. It is, I believe, the Gospel to the Buddhist, who longs for the perfection and peace of an eternal order outside the bounds of human experience, into which he may escape. But he believes that for all but the most heroic and virtuous of men it will take many lives before he can work off the results of wrong living. The risen Christ says that it can be begun, continued and ended in one radical new birth, which certainly demands acceptance and effort, but consists rather of allowing Christ to live within us in all the power of his resurrection. A higher life is available to us through the death of the lower life. We are to be like dead men where sin is concerned, but sensitive and alive in regard to the will and power of God through Christ.

There is more to it than this, for not only can we ourselves become new creatures, but we are called to live in a new order. In the margin of the Revised Version there is an alternative translation—' If any man be in Christ, there is a new creation.' Not only is the man made new, but he is taken into a new order, a new world. This is what happens when we commit ourselves to Christ in baptism ; we are incorporated into the company of the redeemed, the fellowship of the new-born. From this moment on we live in a new order, a new environment, where new laws operate, and new values and new relationships. We look out on the world and our fellow men with new eyes. The world is now God's creation, marred though it may be by man's ignorance and sin. Start anywhere you will in the universe, a blade of grass, the perfection of a flower, a tree in winter or any other season, the wonder of all living things great or small, everything leads to God, every bush is ablaze with his glory.

Saul Kane, the poacher, saw the difference—

> I did not think, I did not strive,
> The deep peace burnt my me alive ;
> The bolted door had broken in,
> I knew that I had done with sin.
> I knew that Christ had given me birth
> To brother all the souls on earth,
> And every bird and every beast
> Should share the crumbs broke at the feast.[1]

Saul Kane was different and so was the world, because Saul was changed and now lived in God's order. The Church in its mission to the world is constantly seeing men become new creatures in a new order. One of the most moving stories of conversion in recent times comes from the Sudan. A Christian in the south, who had become involved in the rebellion which followed independence, was arrested, found guilty of murder and sentenced to death. In prison he was visited by his parish priest and underwent such an experience of penitence and forgiveness that he became a changed man. The change in him was so striking and radiant that six Muslims similarly condemned for murder, came in faith to Christ and were baptized on the eve of their execution. The next morning all seven men, self-confessed murderers, went to the gallows quietly and without fear, penitent for what they had done, but with the peace of forgiven sinners in their hearts, full of hope because they now lived in Christ's order, confident that he was their resurrection and their life.

To live in Christ's new order does not mean that we are saved from all the troubles and sufferings which come to men. In fact, our discipleship may involve us in additional troubles. But in them all there is a new faith

[1] John Masefield, *The Everlasting Mercy* in *Poems* (Heinemann) 1923

and a new power. ' And we know that to them that love
God all things work together for good, even to them that
are called according to his purpose.' This does not mean
that everything that happens is God's perfect will or
that everything happens for the best, but it means that
if we love God and want his will, he will be at work to
bring good out of what seems so painful and disastrous,
something better than if the disastrous thing had never
taken place. S. Paul in an adventurous life for the gospel
underwent many hardships and sufferings—beating,
stoning, imprisonment, shipwreck, hunger and thirst,
spiritual burdens—and he could say,

> Can anything separate us from the love of Christ ?
> Can trouble, pain or persecution ? Can lack of
> clothes and food, danger to life and limb, the threat of
> force of arms ? . . . No, in all these things we win an
> overwhelming victory through Him Who has proved
> His love for us.
> I have become absolutely convinced that neither
> Death nor Life, neither messenger of heaven nor
> monarch of earth, neither what happens today nor
> what may happen tomorrow, neither a power from on
> high nor a power from below, nor anything else in
> God's whole world has any power to separate us from
> the love of God in Jesus Christ our Lord ! [1]

Not just enough strength to get away with things by the
skin of our teeth, but strength and to spare, more than
conquerors. In another magnificently colloquial para-
phrase J. B. Phillips speaks of Christians as ' always being
knocked about but never knocked out.' [2]

The new life in Christ's new order is a life of joy,
adventure and enjoyment, an enlargement. ' For all
things are yours ; whether Paul, or Apollos, or Cephas,

---

[1] J. B. Phillips, *Letters to Young Churches* (Bles)
[2] Ibid.

or the world, or life, or death, or things present, or things
to come ; all are yours : and ye are Christ's ; and Christ
is God's.' ' Everything belongs to you ! . . . For you
belong to Christ, and Christ belongs to God ! ' [1] The
whole world is ours, the whole of life, present and future,
scientific knowledge, artistic beauty, politics and their
use, eating and drinking, sexual love, family life, friendship, justice, nature, the technical world, philosophy in
its true humility as love of wisdom, daring to ask all the
ultimate questions. All belong to us—conditioned only
by one thing, that we belong to Christ, that Christ whose
Cross is foolishness and weakness to the world. We must
not be afraid to accept what is given us, we must not try
to escape life. If we know what it means to be Christ's,
we shall know how to use and control life.[2]

This being in Christ lifts us above all human divisions.
' There can be neither Jew nor Greek, there can be
neither bond nor free, there can be no male or female :
for ye are all one man in Christ Jesus.' The deepest
divisions based on differences of religion and culture are
done away when people enter the new humanity, the
sharpest divisions based on social or economic status no
longer hold, even the difference between the sexes dis-
appears. A new unity comes to those who are in Christ,
for then we all want his will, and so it is as if he were the
only person present : we are all one new man in Christ
Jesus. This was seen very clearly in the early Church,
where slaves and slave owners worshipped together and
listened to S. Paul's words teaching master and slave that
they were members of the same body, sharers in a common
life, both serving the one Lord. So in India caste people
and outcastes learned that when they were incorporated
into Christ they were equal brethren ; untouchability
was washed away in the waters of baptism. So in our

[1] J. B. Phillips, *Letters to Young Churches* (Bles)
[2] See Tillich, *The New Being* (S.C.M. Press)

modern world the fact that people are in Christ should be
the decisive fact in their relationship—Christian Jew and
Christian Arab, Christian Briton and Christian Cypriot
or Egyptian, Christian Indian and Christian Pakistani,
Christian American and Christian Chinese, white Christian and black Christian in South Africa. It is when we
are in Christ that we understand and participate in this
unity at the deepest level. It is right that we should work
for it as an ideal in the political, cultural and social
spheres, yet in one way it is putting the cart before the
horse to try to get racial harmony and world peace as
ends in themselves ; ultimately only in Christ does the
colour of men's skin, nationality, social status, economic
standard cease to exist.

In the book of the Revelation the writer sees ' a new
heaven and a new earth . . . the holy city, new Jerusalem, coming down out of heaven from God, made ready
as a bride adorned for her husband.'

And it is Christ who brings all this about. His
supreme self-revelation in the Apocalypse is in the
image of the Bridegroom, to whom all things are bride.
Wonderful summary ! His grace begins in each a new
life, for the all-renewing Spirit is sent by him, through
whom all things are transfigured. In a transport of
bliss creation hastens to meet him, decked out like a
bride for her husband. (From *The Lord*, by R. Guardini,
Longmans, Green and Co. and the Henry Regnery Co., Chicago.)

PRAYERS

Thou art risen, O Lord !
    Let the gospel trumpets speak,
    and the news as of holy fire,
    burning and flaming and inextinguishable,
    run to the ends of the earth.

Thou art risen, O Lord !
   Let all creation greet the good tidings
      with jubilant shout ;
   for its redemption has come,
    the long night is past, the Saviour lives !
   and rides and reigns in triumph
      now and unto the ages of ages.

E. Milner-White

Spirit of Promise, Spirit of Unity, we thank
Thee that Thou art also the Spirit of Renewal. Renew in the whole Church, we
pray Thee, that passionate desire for the
coming of Thy Kingdom which will unite
all Christians in one mission to the world.
May we all grow up together into Him who
is our Head, the Saviour of the world, and
our only Lord and Master.

Olive Wyon

O Lord Christ, who art the head of the
redeemed humanity, in whom all may find
forgiveness, love and brotherhood, we come
to Thee in gratitude and trust because
Thou hast taken us into Thy new creation.
Help us to rejoice in the fellowship of the
redeemed, seeing in our fellow Christians
those who have been re-born in Thee ; and
in all who know Thee not, those whom
Thou didst die to save and whom Thou
wouldest call to be our brethren. Glory to
Thee, O Blessed Saviour, now and through
all ages.

G. A.

CHAPTER IV

CHRIST IN THE CHRISTIAN

BEFORE Pentecost, Christ was with his disciples—an inspiring teacher and friend, but external to them. Looking back from their fulness of faith they saw those days of his incarnate life as Emmanuel, God *with* men. After Pentecost they found that he was not only with them in a spiritual way as he had promised, ' Lo, I am with you alway,' but he was *within* them, he lived in them. Formerly they had spoken about him, now they spoke through him. In the Resurrection, Ascension and Pentecost the Christ whom they had known in the flesh became spiritualized and transfigured, released by the power of God from all physical limitations into the freedom of pure activity. He had been God with men, now he was God in men.

Warning his disciples of the coming withdrawal of his physical presence, he had promised, ' I will not leave you desolate : I come unto you. . . . In that day ye shall know that I am in my Father, and ye in me, and I in you.' Sometimes he speaks of the Holy Spirit as another : ' I will pray the Father, and he shall give you another Comforter,' whom they shall know, ' for he abideth with you and shall be in you '. The New Testament is clear that God's personality is of a higher and richer order than ours, equally clear about the eternal relationships within the Being of God expressed in the terms Father, Son and Holy Spirit, but it is as insistent as the Old Testament on the unity of God. We Christians often speak of Father, Son and Holy Spirit as if they were three individuals, with the result that non-Christians, especially

Muslims, are puzzled, and as already mentioned accuse us of believing in three Gods. The New Testament speaks of the Holy Spirit, of the Spirit of God and of the Spirit of Jesus ; all these terms mean the same—God in men, Christ in the believer. ' If a man love me, he will keep my word : and my Father will love him, and we will come unto him, and make our abode with him.' The purpose of the Eternal God increases in wonder—God has created man, God has become man, God wills to be in every man. It is through God in us that we recognize that we are his children not only by creation, but by adoption and indwelling. ' God sent forth the Spirit of his Son into our hearts, crying, Abba, Father,' using the affectionate, intimate word ' Abba ' which Christ himself used.

S. Paul speaks of Christ living in him : ' I have been crucified with Christ ; yet I live ; and yet no longer I, but Christ liveth in me : and that life which I now live in the flesh I live in faith, the faith which is in the Son of God, who loved me, and gave himself up for me.' This is not a privilege reserved to S. Paul and the Apostles, it is meant for all Christians : ' But if the Spirit of him that raised up Jesus from the dead dwelleth in you, he that raised up Christ Jesus from the dead shall quicken also your mortal bodies through his Spirit that dwelleth in you.' Paul claimed that his special call was ' to make known what is the riches of the glory of this mystery among the Gentiles, which is Christ in you, the hope of glory.'

In S. John's Gospel Jesus speaks of the relationship between himself and his disciples as that of the vine to its branches. As the branches are part of the vine, so we are united with Christ. As the sap flows into every branch and twig, so the life of Christ flows into every disciple. ' Abide in me, and I in you.' If we do not remain in him and he in us, we cannot bear spiritual fruit ; '. . . apart from me ye can do nothing.'

In the great prayer which Jesus offered before he left the upper room, he prayed for his disciples and for all who should believe through their preaching ' that they may all be one ; even as thou, Father, art in me, and I in thee, that they also may be in us. . . . I in them, and thou in me . . . that the love wherewith thou lovedst me may be in them, and I in them.'

Words of wonder passing wonder—
but thine own, O Truth, O Word of GOD !
Pledge of communion and union with thyself
passing the bond of friend and friend,
of parent and child,
of husband and wife,
though these are love ;
passing the union of body and soul,
though these are one ;
Closer, closest, is the union of Spirit and spirit. . . .[1]

Christ's living in the believer is to be the essence of Christian existence in general.

. . . Let us examine more closely this curious thing called existence. The word means more than mere being ; it means that I am myself and no other ; I alone inhabit me, and no one can enter my habitation unless I open to him. In hours of spiritual plenitude and vitality I feel that I have myself well in hand, that I am master of myself. Herein lies my freedom and dignity, but also the ponderousness and solitude of my existence. We are speaking of purely human existence. To this Paul says : Christian existence is all this and more. Something has changed. Christian personality is not only the natural personality of an individual, but in addition to the solitude and freedom, the dignity and responsibility of the person, there is something else, someone else, Christ.[2]

[1] E. Milner-White, *My God, My Glory* (S.P.C.K.)
[2] R. Guardini, *The Lord* (Longmans and the Henry Regnery Co., Chicago)

Christ and I are still distinct personalities. There is no suggestion of the identity of the human soul and the Universal Soul, of the spirit of man and the Spirit of God. The Hindu religion teaches that the self in man is not merely the divine Self showing itself at one point, it *is* the divine self whole and complete. A Hindu believes that he has attained to full spiritual freedom when he can say with understanding and conviction, ' I am That,' i.e. ' I am God.' He believes, as the Unitarian does, that when Christ said, ' I and the Father are one,' he was not saying something unique about himself, but something which every man should be able to say. The Hindu *swami*, who presides over the Ramakrishna Centre in London, speaking at a recent public meeting said that just as the water in many vessels was all of the same entity, but separated into vessels, so the spirit in men was all part of the divine spirit. Christians believe that man at his highest and holiest is far removed from the holy and eternal God, that he is still a creature, sinful and in need of salvation, but that God in his love and mercy comes to live in him. Here is the perfect union of God the Eternal Being with the being to whom he has given life, personality and freedom, a union far surpassing the absorption of the human spirit into the impersonal cosmic spirit, where all identity is lost and all personal relationships are nothing more than illusion. If Christians could speak more clearly of God within, Hindus might examine the Gospel more hopefully for they have a great longing for union with the divine. Tilak, the Marathi Christian poet, himself a convert from Hinduism, had a deep understanding of union with Christ :

> As the moon and its beams are one,
>   So that I be one with Thee,
> This is my prayer to Thee, my Lord,
>   This is this beggar's plea.

As words and their meaning are linked,
    Serving one purpose each,
Be Thou and I so knit, O Lord,
    And through me breathe Thy speech.

Take Thou this body, O my Christ,
    Dwell as its soul within ;
To be an instant separate
    I count a deadly sin.[1]

The Christ who comes to live in the Christian is still the Christ who came to Bethlehem and who accepted Calvary. He does not and will not force himself on men : ' Behold, I stand at the door and knock : if any man hear my voice and open the door, I will come in to him, and will sup with him, and he with me.' Although it is he who has given man his being, yet he is a courteous and gracious Lord, who knocks at the door of man's soul and patiently waits until the owner is willing to open it.

' Know ye not that ye are a temple of God, and that the Spirit of God dwelleth in you ? ' asks S. Paul of the Christians in Corinth. In spite of all the loving intimacy which our Lord promises, his coming cannot but show up the poor mean lodging that most of us have to offer. Yet he comes, and his very presence shows the things that must go, if he is to stay, and the things that are needed to make him welcome. Zacchaeus was probably a fussy, self-important tax gatherer, who had made his money in ways not always too honest. But for some reason he was eager to see Jesus pass by and, being too short to see over the shoulders of those who lined the road into Jericho, he climbed a tree to make sure of a good view. Somehow Jesus sensed what was in his mind and looking up said to him, ' Zacchaeus, make haste, and come down, for today I must abide at thy house.' It was a very different man who said good-bye to Jesus an hour or two later, a

[1] *Bhakti Niranjana*, by D. N. Tilak (Nagarik Press, Nasik)

humble, grateful, penitent man, whose life from that day onward was going to be different. 'Behold, Lord, the half of my goods I give to the poor ; and if I have wrongfully exacted aught of any man, I restore fourfold.' Salvation had come to the home of Zacchaeus that day, and perhaps for the first time he felt that he was a true son of Abraham rather than a despised outsider. When the Lord comes to his temple, there cannot but be self-judgment, but there is also joy, forgiveness, new life.

This being in Christ and having Christ in us involves us in his sufferings ; indeed, S. Paul tells us that only if we suffer with him shall we share his glory, and that ' as the sufferings of Christ abound unto us, even so our comfort also aboundeth through Christ.' We often wonder how the martyrs managed to endure drawn-out torture and painful death for the sake of Christ, without yielding, without resentment and without self-pity. The answer can only be that the Christ for whom they were suffering was in them to strengthen them in faithfulness unto death. Recent years have shown us that people of all races can face pain and death, and that martyrs did not cease when the Roman Empire decided to make the profession of Christianity no longer a crime against the state. The long list of Kikuyu martyrs shows how African Christians today are ready to suffer for their Lord, and how Christ in them has enabled them to stand firm. Christ in us sooner or later involves us in some kind of costly witness, but he also involves us in his power, so that every faithful follower, however humble, can say with S. Paul, ' I can do all things through Christ which strengtheneth me.'

Modern methods of propaganda and ' brain-washing ' have raised a vital question for Christians : how can the human spirit, however courageous, hold out against the use of drugs, marathon cross-examination, subtle psychological manipulation, under which the power of conscious thought must inevitably break down ? Much will depend on how far the Christian has allowed the Christ in him to penetrate into the deepest levels of the subconscious, into the very springs of personality. R. W. Ford, a young Briton captured by the Chinese in Tibet, spent over four years in a Communist prison, during which time every possible effort was made to ' reform ' him. He was accused of espionage and murder. In conversation with the writer he said that it did not require much treatment to make him confess that he had been technically guilty of the first charge, but the idea of murder was so contrary to all his inmost feelings and convictions that its very impossibility saved his sanity. It was Ford's sub-conscious personality, rather than his conscious thinking that brought him safely through his ordeal.

The spirit of man has been created by God and when it is penetrated by the Spirit of the indwelling Christ, layer after layer of his personality is cleansed and renewed, so that even in dreams or unconsciousness his sanctified personality will express itself. The only way to deal with such a man is to kill him, and that in itself is a confession of failure.

In the Sacrament of Holy Communion our Lord has given us something which not only shows us how he wills to be assimilated into us, but also a means of feeding and strengthening our spiritual life. The words in his teaching after the feeding of the five thousand are startling and almost crudely materialistic : ' I am the bread of life . . . he that eateth my flesh and drinketh my blood abideth in me, and I in him.' We can go with him that far, but he takes us still farther, ' As the living Father sent me, and I live because of the Father ; so *he that eateth me*, he also shall live because of me.' As material food assimilated by the body gives life, health and strength to the whole body, so the life of the Risen Lord accepted by faithful disciples is assimilated into every level of the spiritual life. Christ wills to live in the Christian. Just as the spirit of man is the shaper of his body, so Christ is the shaper of body and soul. And when he is within us, then the process is begun by which we grow to complete spiritual maturity, ' unto a fullgrown man, unto the measure of the stature of the fulness of Christ.'

The doctrine of the Holy Spirit in man should come as gospel to Hindus yearning for union with God, and to the mystics of all religions who try through meditation to enter into direct touch with him. It comes with an even greater sense of good news to animists, who believe that this world is penetrated by the action of spiritual beings— spirits of nature, spirits of disease, spirits of the dead. Most of these spirits are looked upon with fear, as spirits who have to be propitiated or outwitted or induced by sacrifices and magical means to work for the benefit of the worshipper or to the harm of his enemies. Often in Asia or Africa a man will become possessed by an evil spirit who will drive him demented, or he will worry himself to breakdown or death through fear of the witchdoctor's magic.

There are two points in the Christian understanding of God's operation which make up the gospel to those who live in the grip of evil spirits. In the Gospels they see numerous examples of Christ casting out evil spirits and making men whole. They read of Christ sending out the twelve to heal the sick, cleanse the lepers and cast out devils, and of the return of the seventy, who rejoiced that even the devils were subject to them in Christ's name. S. Paul speaks of Christ's victory over all principalities and powers : all the spiritual powers are subject to Christ, the good ones because of their obedience, the evil ones because of the victory of his Cross.

From every part of the Church come reports of men's deliverance from the power and fear of evil spirits through the power of Christ. In villages in the Irrawaddy delta, when a person falls ill, a pig or a chicken is offered to the offended spirits. If this is not effective, all the members of the family are summoned to take part in a sacrificial meal, which is not regarded as effective if one member is absent. If there is a Christian in the family, he feels himself torn between loyalty to Christ and love of his family and the sick member. What a great day it will be when all the members of the family can gather in the Holy Communion, partaking of the spiritual food which shall preserve body and soul unto eternal life, holding the loved one up to the healing love and power of God, trusting in the divine will for his highest good, confident that in life or death we belong to God, and nothing can pluck us out of his hand !

Secondly, the animist accepts naturally the inter-action of the spiritual and the material, and this is some-thing which can prepare him for belief in God who is Spirit, who created the world, who was incarnated in it and who indwells it with his Spirit. Think of the joy when the animist discovers that the Spirit, of which he has always been so conscious but also so afraid, is the Spirit of holiness and love, the Spirit of Jesus Christ.

We have already thought of Christ's victory over death. The spirits of the dead are in his keeping ; S. Paul tells us that our Lord went down to the kingdom of the dead to proclaim his victory to those who had died before his coming. We believe that his power and love can reach them there. Primitive people are conscious of their continuity with their ancestors, as are also the Chinese. The Christian belief in the Communion of Saints, that kinship in Christ which includes the living and the dead, is the crown of the Gospel.

I believe that Christ's Kingdom extends over paradise, that through him we can send our love to the dead, that even there he will seek out the sheep lost through its own foolishness, the coin lost by accident, the son lost through

wilfulness, the penitent thief, the impenitent one, poor
remorseful Judas, you and me, and all those who in this
life never had the opportunity of learning of his saving
love.

PRAYERS

O Spirit of God
   who dost speak to spirits
      created in thine own likeness :
Penetrate into the depths of our spirits,
   into the storehouse of memories
      remembered or forgotten,
into the very springs of personality,
   and cleanse
      and forgive.

G. A.

Christ be with me, Christ within me,
Christ behind me, Christ before me,
Christ beside me, Christ to win me,
Christ to comfort and restore me,
Christ beneath me, Christ above me,
Christ in quiet, Christ in danger,
Christ in hearts of all that love me,
Christ in mouth of friend and stranger.

S. Patrick's Breastplate

This is my Lord,
   beside and about me,
      coming and entering and abiding within.
This is my Lord, to whom I belong :
This, my Lord, calling me nearer and nearer.

This is my Lord, who died for me :
This, my Lord, who taketh away my sin :
This, my Lord, clothing me in his righteousness :
This, my Lord, giving strength for today and
   tomorrow :

This, my Lord, with his own hands feeding me
   with his own life,
   with his Body and his Blood,
   with his heart and his soul.

As he would dwell in me,
   may I dwell in him
     for ever and ever.

E. Milner-White

CHAPTER V

CHRIST IN THE CHURCH

THE disciples of Christ, however holy each one may become through the indwelling Christ, are not expected to remain as isolated individuals but to be welded together into a community of holiness and love, which will be shaped and indwelt by Christ as the individual is. The Church is not just the aggregate of all the individual believers ; she is the visible corporate expression of Christ's presence. After the Ascension the earliest disciples did not call a meeting and say to one another, ' We must not let the knowledge of the Lord Jesus Christ die out, we must keep the faith alive, let us therefore form a society to carry on his aims.' The Church was there, it was something given. Something in existence before Christians, something into which Christians had to enter. At Caesarea Philippi, Jesus blessed Peter for his confession that he was the Christ, and said that ' upon this rock '—of the divine revelation of Jesus as God's Christ—' I will build my church ; and the gates of hell shall not prevail against it.' As the Church goes out in his Name the forces of hell and death shall not be able to withstand its invasion, the gates shall be broken down and the prisoners freed.

On the first Easter evening the Risen Lord commissions his disciples to carry on his mission to the world : ' " As the Father has sent me, even so I send you." And when he had said this, he breathed on them, and said to them, " Receive the Holy Spirit." ' [1] His Spirit was to be their life, just as breath had been the life of his body.

[1] From *The Holy Bible, Revised Standard Version* (Thos. Nelson & Sons Ltd), John, 20, 21–2

S. Matthew records a later repetition of the commission :
' All authority hath been given unto me in heaven and
on earth. Go ye therefore, and make disciples of all the
nations . . . and lo, I am with you alway, even unto the
end of the world.' The Church is thus ' the-way-in-which-
Jesus-Christ-continues-to-live-and-to-act-upon-earth-for-
man's-salvation.' [1]

That it was the Spirit of Christ active in the Church is
seen on the day of Pentecost when 3,000 souls were converted and baptized, an event of unexpected magnitude,
quite beyond unaided human achievement. 'And the Lord
added to them day by day those that were being saved.'

S. Paul speaks of the Church as the Body of Christ.
When our Lord was here on earth he acted through his
own body—speaking with his own voice, journeying
through the villages of Galilee on his own feet, laying his
own hands on the sick. Now he does all these things
through the Church, which is to the Risen Christ what
his body was to the incarnate Jesus. We must never make
the mistake of separating Christ and his Church. Without
the Church we should know nothing about Christ. It
is the Church that collected the books of the New Testament and gave them its seal of authenticity and authority ;
it is the Church that drew up the creeds as a summary of
faith. It is into the Church that we are incorporated at
our baptism. The Church is part of the Gospel : it is
part of the Christian creed.

You cannot be a Christian in isolation. You cannot
call God ' Father, my Father,' without also saying,
' Father, our Father.' You cannot love God only, you
must also love your neighbour. The Church is Jesus
Christ and his circle, and that circle is like an electric
circuit in which the current will only flow when one hand
is in the hand of Jesus Christ and the other in the hand of
the brother in Christ.

[1] Douglas Edwards, C.R., *The Necessity of the Church* (Mirfield)

The Church, as it goes out into the world to carry on Christ's saving work, calls to all men to come and join the brotherhood of God's family, the fellowship of the redeemed, the community of love. There should be no distinctions of race in the Church, no differences of class, no warmer welcome to the wealthy members than to the poorest, no greater value attached to the man in high position than to the humblest member. No member of Christ's Church should ever be allowed to feel lonely ; his relatives may have died, friends may have moved away, in the Church he should be able to find a home and a welcome. The newcomer should be able to come to the local Christian community as the most natural thing in the world. When a West Indian or a West African comes to live in the neighbourhood, he should be almost embarrassed by the number of friendly calls and the offers of service. The Christian student from overseas, whatever may be the colour of his skin, ought to find no difficulty in securing lodging in a Christian home, and no non-Christian should be allowed to return to his own country without feeling that he has lived among friends.

Within this community of love, the newcomer to baptism, whether child or adult, should know that the whole community is concerned and glad, the sick should feel supported by the prayers of the rest, those in trouble or even in disgrace should feel the concern of all, those facing some problem or embarking on a new adventure should feel strengthened by the common desire that the good will of the Lord be done.

S. Paul in his teaching about the Church as a body says that ' the members should have the same care one for another. And whether one member suffereth, all the members suffer with it ; or one member is honoured, all the members rejoice with it.' ' All that you do,' said the great Cardinal Mercier in one of his pastoral letters, ' for good or evil, either benefits or damages the whole society of souls. The humblest of souls in the most obscure situation can, through the degree of virtue at which it lives and the work it is called to do, make its contribution to the general sanctification of the Church.' [1]

If one member can influence the strength or weakness of the whole body, how much more should local Christian communities and whole churches be able to support other local communities and churches needing reinforcement of spiritual strength. Deep down in our spiritual unity in Christ there can pass movements of love, power and prayer from one part of the Church to the other. After the fall of Burma a Burmese priest listening to the B.B.C. on a clandestine radio set happened to tune in to a great service, which was being broadcast from London and in which Christians were remembering and praying for their brethren in S.E. Asia. He said he realized as never before the spiritual unity of the Church and the power of loving prayer. Throughout the world there has been a faithful outpouring of prayer for the Church in China, some of it no doubt telling God what he ought to do about it, but all prompted by a love of the brethren ; we may never know the full effect of this volume of prayer. Bishop Ting during his visit to Britain in 1956 thanked the Church in the west for its prayer for China, and added with a delightful touch of humour and insight, ' God has listened to your prayers with a grain of salt.' We have only the right to pray that God's will may be done and in God's own way, which often will not be our way, trusting in the promise that the gates of hell shall not prevail.

All that has been said so far has concerned Christ's will for his Church, the ideal that we see set forth in the New Testament. We cannot but be conscious of how sadly the Church fails to live up to the Church of the Lord. There are many people, with the deepest reverence for Christ, who feel reluctant to link up with the Church.

[1] Quoted in Evelyn Underhill, *Collected Papers* (Longmans)

To them the Church is an obstacle. They do not accept Christ as Lord because they do not see Christ in those who bring the Gospel to them. Christianity has spread with the invasion of the rest of the world by the white race ; it has often been mixed up with western imperialism, even though it has done much to moderate the worst effects of that expansion. Asian peoples have been hindered by our Britishness, and perhaps by their own nationalism, aroused in reaction. The Church must be seen to be truly universal, yet expressing itself as indigenous in each country, no longer a hot-house plant brought from a foreign country, but rooted in its own soil. The faith in Jesus Christ as God and Saviour and Lord of the whole Church will be the same everywhere, but in its expression in worship and character it will reflect the genius of its own people, so that the Church will no longer appear foreign ; it too will be universal, yet always bearing the marks of a colony of heaven.

Another hindrance in the minds of thinking people in Asia is the organized power of the Christian Church, with its immense resources in money and buildings. The local church has often a desperate struggle to pay its way and give its share, but in its total possessions the Christian Church must be the richest corporation in the world ; often the thought of the Church's power fails to remind men of the Christ of the Gospels. There is another subtle danger in the organized constitutional life of the Church : in the committee of a local church or the governing body of a group of churches or a denomination, almost every one of its members may be a person of integrity and devotion, yet there is the temptation of the group to carry over into church business the methods and standards of the world, so that the corporate life of the Church is not seen as the corporate expression of the life of its Lord.

Undeveloped Christianity is another hindrance, the

fact that so many Christians seem to live in the Old Testament with its pre-Christian ideas, rather than in the New Testament where Christ has preserved for us all that is true and eternal in the long education of the people of God, and has rejected or corrected all that he saw as men's mistaken ideas. The Old Testament must ever be read in the light of Christ ; we Christians start with Christ and judge everything by him.

Mahatma Gandhi had a great reverence for Christ, the Sermon on the Mount was his constant study ; at the end of each of his great fasts he asked for the hymn, ' When I survey the wondrous cross.' Yet he never accepted Christ as Lord and God. He was once asked by the great American missionary, Stanley Jones, what advice he would give to a Christian missionary about to begin work in India. His reply was : ' Be a little more like your Jesus. Teach your converts that when they become Christians they do not cease to be Indians. Don't water down your religion, don't reduce your demands, hold your people up to the highest.'

One of the greatest obstacles in bringing the world to Christ is the divided Church. It is puzzling enough to Christians in Asia and Africa ; they see that we all worship the one God, that we have all been saved by the one Christ, all admitted into the new creation by him, all nourished by him, that we all use the same Bible and confess the same faith. Yet we are divided. Our disunity is even more puzzling to the non-Christians to whom we are trying to present the Gospel. Our Lord prayed that his disciples might be one so that the world might believe that the Father had sent him ; in other words, the world's acceptance of Christ as Lord depends, humanly speaking, on the unity of Christians.

We can thank God that the conscience of the whole Church is being awakened to the stumbling-block of our divisions ; we can thank God for the heroic adventure

in unity of the Church of South India, and for the schemes
of union in North India, Ceylon, Nigeria ; we can be
grateful for the growing volume of prayer that the Church
may become one according to the will of Christ and in
the way that Christ himself shall choose ; and deeply
thankful that it was a Roman Catholic priest, the Abbé
Couturier, who taught so many to pray in this way.
Above all, we can praise God for the younger Churches
who never cease to tell us that, whereas unity may be
desirable in the lands of the older Churches, it is absol-
utely imperative in their own lands, if they are to present
Christ to the millions of people in Asia with any hope of
acceptance.　It is we in the west who are putting the
brake on the progress towards unity. The conversations
between Anglicans and Presbyterians, and between
Methodists and Anglicans, and the Vatican's call for an
ecumenical council—these surely show a growing obedience to the promptings of the Holy Spirit.　Let there be
urgency in our thinking and praying : ' Forgetting the
things which are behind, and stretching forward to the
things that are before.'　Let us be eager to discover our
fellow-Christians in each local situation ; let us press
the Assemblies, the Conferences, the Unions to make
unity the priority that it was in the mind of Christ ; and
let us be sure that the only thing that holds up Christ's
gift of unity is the lukewarmness of our desire for it.

A welcome step forward was taken by the 1958 Lambeth Conference of the Bishops of the Anglican Communion, when, dealing with reunion plans for Ceylon
and for North India and Pakistan, it advised ' that when
Churches have been united in such a way that the whole
ministry of the United Church has been episcopally
united, permission to visiting ministers, not episcopally
ordained, of Churches in communion with the United
Churches at the time of union, to celebrate the Holy
Communion occasionally when visiting a United Church,

be not regarded as a bar to relations of full communion between the United Church and the Churches and Provinces of the Anglican Communion ; provided that due constitutional provisions are made to safeguard the conscience of worshippers.' [1] This departure from Anglican practice recognizes that anomalies are bound to continue until reunion progresses further in other parts of the world ; in effect, it recognizes that disunion is the greatest anomaly of all.

More and more people from all the Churches, and notably in the Roman Catholic and Greek Orthodox Churches, are beginning to take part in the Week of Prayer for Christian Unity, held in January each year. Yet we must beware lest we think that we have done all that is necessary when we have prayed for something. We cannot expect our Lord to answer our prayers, unless we have done all within our own power to bring about the end for which we are praying.

As we consider the present state of the Church, however, can we with any degree of honesty say that it is in any way the hope of the world ? It may well be in our thinking ; it is certainly so in the purpose of Christ, but is it so in the thinking of the nations ? Do the nations of Asia, with four out of every five people not getting enough food to eat, look to the Church as their hope and champion ? Can South Africa, with its desperate need of racial unity, look for power from a Church which is divided into nine hundred different sects and separatist bodies ? Is the Church still the body that turns the world upside down so that for once it is right way up ? Probably more people are looking to Communism and are ready to sacrifice freedom for food, in order to escape from the prison of hunger and under-privilege. As the Spirit of man is to his body, as Christ in the Christian re-creates man as God means him to be, as Christ in the

[1] *The Lambeth Conference, 1958* (S.P.C.K.) Part I, p. 36

Church shapes the Church, so the Church is meant by him to be the creative, shaping influence in the world, the pattern of how men should live together. Yeast in the loaf, salt in the pot of rice or vegetables, a city set on a hill, a light in a dark place. Is the Church that to the world ?

Critics of the Christian Church are vigorous in pointing out the sins of the Church all down the ages—the heresies and schisms, the periods of worldliness and deadness, the wars of religion, the Inquisition, the denominational rivalries, the failure to lead the nations into the way of peace, the seeming failure of the Church in western countries to influence the policies of their countries towards other countries. Dr. Radhakrishnan's criticism applies equally to Churches as to individuals ' You Christians make such extraordinary claims, but you are such ordinary people.' It was once said many centuries ago that the Christians in the Roman Empire out-lived (in quality, not longevity), out-died, out-thought their contemporaries. How can we once again recapture that creative spirit ?

The saving hope is that the Church should always hold itself under the judgment of its Lord. If the Lord is truly in the Temple of his Church, he will be like a refiner's fire, like the red-hot furnace in a smelting factory ; he will purify clergy and people alike, ' For the time is come for judgment to begin at the house of God. . . .' The Nicene Creed gives us four marks of the Church to which we give our loyal assent—one . . . holy . . . Catholic . . . and Apostolic . . . Church. One, with the unity of the indwelling Christ ; holy, with the forgiveness of Christ and with his holiness ; Catholic, with the fulness of the truth as it is in Him, and with his love for all men ; Apostolic—sent by him into the world, into every situation, to identify itself with the sufferings, sins and needs of men and to mediate his saving love and power.

The Church is the company of all faithful believers in Jesus Christ ; Christ means it to be the community of love in which we not only love our neighbours as ourselves but try to love them as he loves us ; it is a fellowship of forgiven and forgiving people ; it is the sphere of the Holy Spirit's operation ; it is a family in which we hold up one another to the highest and in which we speak the truth to one another in love. It is perhaps nearest to Christ's ideal for it in its compassion for suffering people, in its care for the sick, in its efforts for the millions of homeless refugees in Central Europe, in the land of our Lord's birth, in Hong Kong and other places ; in its stand for racial brotherhood against white *apartheid* in South Africa or black fanaticism in Kenya ; in its protests against tyranny and exploitation ; in its rôle as watchman to warn men of things that will destroy their spiritual life ; in its effort to rescue the prostitute in East London, or to show the teddy boy that life can be full of adventure, friendliness and joy in living. The Church has the keys of the Kingdom of Heaven in its keeping, and wherever it proclaims the gospel in life as well as word, men will knock at its doors.

With all its faults the Church is part of the Gospel, and as it holds itself humbly, persistently, yet lovingly, under the judgment and guidance of its Lord, men will ultimately recognize it as such. We cannot do better than continue to pray the prayer that has been prayed in the Church all down the years since Pope Gelasius included it in his prayer book about the year 500 :

O Lord, we beseech thee, let thy continual pity cleanse and defend thy Church ; and, because it cannot continue in safety without thy succour, preserve it evermore by thy help and goodness ; through Jesus Christ our Lord.

PRAYERS

O God, mighty to save, infinite in compassion towards the nations that know thee not, and the tongues which cannot speak thy name : We humbly thank thee that thou hast made the Church of thy dear Son the chariot of the Gospel, to tell it out among the nations that thou art king, and to bear thy love unto the world's end ; and for all thy servants who counted not their lives dear unto them on this employment, and for all peoples newly praising thee, we praise and bless thee, Father, Son and Holy Spirit, one Lord and God for ever and ever. -

E. Milner-White

Most gracious Father, we humbly beseech Thee, for Thy Holy Catholic Church. Fill it with all truth ; in all truth with all peace. Where it is corrupt, purge it ; where it is in error, direct it ; where anything is amiss, reform it ; where it is right, strengthen and confirm it ; where it is in want, furnish it ; where it is divided and rent asunder, make up the breaches of it, O Thou Holy One of Israel.

Archbishop Laud

Almighty God, whose Son Jesus Christ came to cast fire upon the earth : grant that by the prayers and labours of thy faithful people a fire of burning zeal may be kindled and pass from heart to heart, that the light of thy Church may shine forth bright and clear to all mankind, through the same Thy Son, Jesus Christ our Lord.

William Bright

CHAPTER VI

THE ETERNAL CHRIST

DEEPLY as we believe Christ to be in the individual Christian and in the divine society of the Church, deeply as we have experienced him in these two spheres, deeply as we are committed to carry on his saving work through the world mission of the Church, we cannot limit his activity to the Church only. The prophets of the Old Testament were emphatic that God was at work in history, active in the rise and fall of empires, turning the very rebellions of men to his purpose ; chastening his own people through historic happenings to be more worthy of the purpose revealed to Abraham, the father of the faithful, ' in thee shall all the families of the earth be blessed '.

Arnold Toynbee in his great *Study of History* gives a very graphic account of how one civilization after another rises and then falls because it has within it the seeds of its own decay. Looked at from the Biblical viewpoint each civilization fails to recognize the things that belong unto peace and the time of its visitation, expressed in moments of opportunity and judgment. The upheavals in history are all signs that God is marching on in his purpose : ' When these things begin to come to pass, look up, and lift up your heads ; because your redemption draweth nigh.' In every upheaval God's purpose is advanced a stage further. But the end is not yet, for ' This gospel of the kingdom shall be preached in the whole world for a testimony unto all the nations ; and then shall the end come.'

If we believe that God is at work in history, surely we

must also believe that he is active in the religious experience of men, and not only through the Christian mission. The ancient religions have been stirred to new activity by the spirit of nationalism which is the dominant force in Asia and Africa today, which makes people in every country focus their attention on their own history, culture and the traditional religion to which they have given their allegiance in the past. Statesmen in each newly independent nation look to the ancient religion not only to be a unifying spiritual force but also a source of inspiration for the exciting period of history ahead. Leaders of the other religions are conscious of the mess into which the world has fallen and are eager to show that their own religion is the one best qualified to rescue it. The result is that vigorous attempts are being made to prevent people becoming Christians in their own countries, and missions are being sent out to other countries. There are a number of Muslim mosques in Britain, Buddhist missionaries are at work, there is a Ramakrishna Vedanta Centre in London and Hindu *swamis* frequently give public lectures on eastern philosophy and meditation. The other religions are awake and active as they have not been for centuries, and the real encounter between them and Christianity is now about to take place. This raises in our minds the question, ' What is God doing in the other religions ? '

In a recent article in *The Daily Telegraph*,[1] Dr. W. R. Matthews, the Dean of S. Paul's, deals with this problem :

> The question is bound to arise in the mind of any intelligent Christian, where does my faith stand in reference to the other great religions ? On the whole, the answer given by the Church in the past has been that Christianity is the true religion and all others are simply false.

[1] See ' The Summing Up ' by Dr. W. R. Matthews in *The Daily Telegraph*, 16th August, 1958.

The enlarged knowledge which we now have of the history of religion and of the sacred books of other faiths render this answer unacceptable, and I suppose that most of us would be prepared to admit that the quests for God that have produced the higher religions have not been wholly in vain and that the Holy Spirit has been at work in other spheres as well as in the Hebrew people and the Christian Church.

The writer of the fourth Gospel speaks of Christ as ' the light which lighteth every man ' and commenting on this statement Archbishop Temple says, ' All that is noble in non-Christian systems of thought, or conduct, or worship is the work of Christ upon them and within them. By the Word of God—that is to say, by Jesus Christ—Isaiah, and Plato, and Zoroaster, and Buddha, and Confucius conceived and uttered such truths as they declared. There is only one divine light ; and every man in his measure is enlightened by it.' [1] If Christ is the Truth, then all truth must come from him.

This thought is supported by S. Paul's teaching in the Epistle to the Ephesians of God's purpose ' to sum up all things in Christ '. This verse is often interpreted as meaning that God plans to gather all men together into Christ ; surely it must also mean that in the end all spiritual movements will be reconciled and fulfilled in Christ.

Zoroaster was a Persian who lived about 600 B.C. He believed in one God, the creator and sustainer of the universe, who is just and good, and who has given free will to all men. He believed that man was designed by God to be immortal in body and soul, and that he was endowed by God with conscience and will, and thus able to choose between good and evil. Zoroaster also believed in an evil spirit, in revolt against God and who is evil by choice rather than by nature. History is a never-ending

[1] William Temple, *Readings in S. John's Gospel* (Macmillan)

struggle between the righteous God and the Evil Spirit. After the inevitable defeat of the Devil the new heaven and earth will come into existence and men will enjoy eternal fellowship with God. Here was a man whose faith was very close to that of the great Hebrew prophets ; in his belief in immortal life he was in advance of them. How do we account for Zoroaster in the eternal providence of God and in his revelation of himself through the Eternal Christ ? [1]

The Buddha (560–480 B.C.) was one of the great spiritual and moral giants of all time. He lived in a great spiritual freedom from the chains that bind most men, he had a wonderful compassion and love for all men, he saw with clear insight that man's great need was to get free from all desire, greed, craving and attachment, and he believed that this could be done by men exerting their own wills to live a life of true virtue. How do we Christians explain this great religious genius who can well be included in the very small group of ' the greatest born of woman ' ? Are we to write him off simply as a rival of Christ, who is ultimately to be displaced by Christ ? Or are we to see the pre-incarnate Christ, the Eternal Christ, the Word who was always with God, at work in him ?

And what about Mohammed ? Here was a man in the true tradition of Abraham, who in an Arabia full of belief in jinns, spirits, and idols, came to believe in the One True God, a man who believed that he heard God speaking to him and tried to express through his great spirit the experience of God which had come to him. Do we so reserve God's activity to Jews before Christ and Christians after Christ that we deny any spiritual reality to the experience of Mohammed, or do we believe that the Eternal Christ was in some way working with him ?

This does not mean that the other religions will in time develop into Christianity, but that God is at work

[1] See R. C. Zaehner, *At Sundry Times* (Faber & Faber Ltd.)

within them in such a way that there are pointers to his supreme revelation in Jesus Christ. When faith in Christ comes, these pointers will be seen to have been fulfilled in him, and so will be in the nature of good news and fulfilment. Yet there is much in the other religions which is the product of human thinking only, and some of this will finally be seen to be incomplete or untrue. All religions cannot be true because there are so many things in the different religions which cancel one another out.

There was much in the teaching of both the Buddha and the Prophet which reflected their own times and personalities, much that was incomplete, some to be corrected. Even that greatest of all Christian missionaries, S. Paul, warned us that ' we have this treasure in earthen vessels ' : our own experience of God-in-Christ has to be interpreted to ourselves, then it has to be expressed in human words to others, and in the process it inevitably falls short of God's intention and truth.

This thought raises the problem of how we are to interpret our faith in Christ and our experience of him to people of other faiths. In itself it is something spiritual and intangible, yet it has to be put into words, and words which must mean the same thing to other people as they do to ourselves. So often we just speak from the point at which we ourselves stand ; somehow we have to put ourselves in the place of our hearers, and relate our message to their situations. God did this in Christ, when he came down into our world, was born as a man, lived the same kind of life that all of us have to live, and showed us in terms of human living what he meant. In the same way we have to relate the Gospel to the experience of people of other faiths, to enter into their thinking, their hopes and longings, until at last we can present it in terms of Buddhism or Islam or Hinduism so that it appears as good news.

That the Church in its mission to the world is beginning

to realize this is shown in the study centres for the approach to the other religions which are being sponsored by the National Christian Councils of Asia and the International Missionary Council. There are study centres in various stages of development in Bangalore for the study of Hinduism, in Colombo and Rangoon for the study of Theravada Buddhism, in the Middle East and in Pakistan and India for the study of Islam, and in Hong Kong for the study of the religious spirit of the Chinese people. The International Missionary Council and the World Council of Churches are co-operating in a study programme under the title ' The Word of God and the Living Faiths of Men ', in which scholars, missionaries and theologians from different races, countries and Churches are trying to trace the footsteps of God as he seeks men and reveals himself to them.

Let me illustrate this new approach in a personal confession. For nearly twenty years I worked as a missionary in Burma. Very early in that period I came to a deep reverence of the Buddha, an appreciation of the high ethical standards of Buddhism, and an admiration of the tolerant, kindly character produced in many devout Buddhists. I met monks whose spirit of quiet detachment spoke of a peace attained through years of discipline and meditation. But all the time I spoke as one outside rather than as one who had incarnated himself in Buddhist life and thought until at length he could speak of Christ in Buddhist ideas as well as in the Burmese language.

To be a missionary to people of other faiths requires listening, patience, time ; it will be months before he is qualified and ready to speak. Till then his task will be to learn, to ask questions, to make friends, with the aim of deeply understanding. This is what S. Paul meant when he said, ' To the Jews I became as a Jew, that I might gain Jews ; to them that are under the law, as under the law ; . . . to them that are without law as without law, not being without law to God, but under law to Christ, that I might gain them that are without law. To the weak I became weak, that I might gain the weak ; I am become all things to all men, that I may by all means save some. And I do all things for the gospel's sake. . . .' There is no watering down or compromise, but the identification of himself with his hearers, in order to communicate the message.

This demand that the Gospel shall be presented in a way that touches the life and thought of the hearers cannot be limited to the other religions. It applies generally. Canon Wickham of Sheffield is never weary of pointing out that the Church in Great Britain is almost completely out of touch with the mass of industrial workers and has been since the Industrial Revolution. He points out that although theologically speaking men may be made in the image of God, yet speaking practically they are fashioned in the image of their craft, and so are the towns they live in. So it is not sufficient to have churches in industrial centres, unless they can relate their thought and life to the function and structure of the industry which is the determining factor in any particular area. The same thought was in the minds of the group of Roman Catholic priests in Paris who, several years ago, decided to earn their own living as factory workers, to live in small flats as the workers did, to say mass in the evening in their homes, giving an open invitation to all who cared to attend. Ernest Southcott, the Vicar of S. Wilfrid's, Halton, Leeds, has the same aim, when on several mornings in the week he goes to a Christian home to celebrate the Holy Communion on the kitchen table, in the presence of neighbours who have been invited by the Christian host. If men will not come to the Church, the Church must go to men, in their work places and in their homes, in the same way that God came to men in Jesus Christ.

Industrialization is proceeding at a great pace in the countries of Asia and Africa today. It is not only in the gold mines of Johannesburg, the copper mines of Rhodesia, the mills of Bombay and the factories of Japan, but new industrial centres are springing up in formerly rural areas in Ghana and Uganda, and life is being changed in the course of a few months from that of a quiet rural village to that of a large, noisy industrial town. The Church has the responsibility of making clear to people in these areas what is happening, and of relating its life to the situation so that Christ is seen as Lord and the Gospel as the key to the right pattern of society.

Unless we present Christ in this relevant way, he will appear to men as a stranger, a foreigner, the friend of a few, instead of God's Word to men of every race and age and in every situation. It is Christ who is our Gospel more than the Christianity in which we have to express and organize our discipleship. Christ is God's answer to men's search for him. Christ is the end of all human systems of religion, he is the God-given religion. If we try to present Christianity as the best of all religions, we are putting Christianity in the same category as other religions. Our task is to present Christ.

Speaking on the text ' For neither circumcision counts for anything, nor uncircumcision, but a new creation ', Professor Tillich asks, ' How shall Christianity face them (the other religions) ? Shall Christianity tell them : Come to us, we are a better religion . . .' Giving a definite negative to this question, he continues :

No religion matters—only a new state of things. Let us think about this striking assertion of Paul. What it says first is that Christianity is more than a religion ; it is the message of a New Creation. . . . Paul says : ' No particular religion matters, neither ours, nor yours. But I want to tell you that something has happened that matters, something that judges you

and me, your religion and my religion. A New
Creation has occurred, a New Being has appeared ;
and we are all asked to participate in it. And so we
should say to the pagans and Jews wherever we meet
them : Don't compare your religion and our religion,
your rites and our rites, your prophets and our prophets,
your priests and our priests, the pious amongst you and
the pious amongst us. All this is of no avail.' And
above all don't think that we want to convert you to
English or American Christianity, to the religion of
the Western World. We do not want to convert you
to us, not even to the best of us. This would be of no
avail. We want only to show you something we have
seen and to tell you something we have heard : That
in the midst of the old creation there is a New Creation,
and that this New Creation is manifest in Jesus who is
called the Christ ! [1]

In the last chapter we saw that the Church is Christ's
creation and that he has committed to her the task of
carrying on his mission ; we also saw how often the
Church is an obstacle to men coming to Christ. If we
start with Christ we are safe—if we start with the Church
or with a vague system that we call Christianity, we are
starting with a secondary matter, which is only in its
right place when it is secondary to Christ. Brought to
Christ men can accept the Church, because they know
that it is his Body, in which he wills to be involved with
all our weaknesses, and also because they will then see
that the Church, when it is trying to be his Body, is ready
to hold itself under his judgment.

When men can see Christ without the Christian or the
Church getting between him and them, they know there
is something about him which attracts and challenges
and pursues them. In his exile on St. Helena Napoleon
had plenty of time to think about his own success and

[1] Tillich, *The New Being* (S.C.M. Press)

failure and about deeper things. He has this unexpected
passage about our Lord :

> Jesus Christ was more than man. . . . I have in-
> spired multitudes with such an enthusiastic devotion
> that they would have died for me . . . but to do this
> it was necessary that I should be visibly present with
> the electric influence of my looks, of my words, of my
> voice. When I saw men and spoke to them, I lighted
> up the flame of self-devotion in their hearts. . . .
> Christ alone has succeeded in so raising the mind of
> man toward the Unseen, that it becomes insensible to
> the barriers of time and space. Across a chasm of
> eighteen hundred years, Jesus Christ makes a demand
> which is beyond all others difficult to satisfy ; he asks
> for that which a philosopher may often seek in vain at
> the hands of his friends, or a father of his children, or
> a bride of her spouse, or a man of his brother. He
> asks for the human heart ; he will have it entirely to
> himself. He demands it unconditionally ; and forth-
> with his demand is granted. Wonderful ! In defiance
> of time and space, the soul of man, with all its powers
> and faculties, becomes an annexation to the empire of
> Christ. All who sincerely believe in him experience
> that supernatural love towards him. This phe-
> nomenon is unaccountable; it is altogether beyond the
> scope of man's creative powers.[1]

It would be a revealing exercise to collect in one
anthology what people who did not accept Jesus as Lord
and God have said about him. It would certainly en-
large our own conception of him. Vinoba Bhave is the
spiritual successor of Mahatma Gandhi, who has walked
up and down India, appealing to land-owners to give him
land to hand over to landless villagers. In a recent speech
he spoke of Jesus as the Son of Man ' and that means he

[1] Quoted from Dr. Liddon's *Bampton Lectures*, by Arthur W. Robinson,
in *The Personal Life of the Clergy* (Longmans)

belongs to us in the east as well as to the western nations '.
Then after speaking of the piling up of armaments by
the so-called Christian nations he proceeded, ' But this
will not go on for many days longer. In accordance with
the hope that Jesus has given, we look forward to the
fulfilment in a short time of his prophecy that God's
Kingdom which is now in heaven will begin to operate
as a Kingdom on earth. Then men will learn to live
together in mutual love and co-operation, and will
experience the joy that comes from giving rather than
getting.' Vinoba Bhave concluded his address : ' In
our conduct there are faults. For them I ask pardon of
the Lord, who will grant us pardon. Jesus forgave those
who nailed him to the Cross. He is extremely forgiving.
Why should he not forgive us ? ' [1]

At a recent meeting in London a Muslim *imam* (leader)
in an address to a gathering of people from different faiths,
quoted three times from the words of Jesus in the Gospels.
After the meeting I said to him how moved I had been
at hearing Christ's words quoted so reverently and aptly
by a man from another faith. Putting a hand on my
shoulder the *imam* replied, ' My dear friend, when you
Christians think that you have a monopoly of Jesus it
hurts us Muslims, for we think that he belongs to everybody.' My Muslim friend may not be near what we
would call conversion to Christianity, but he was coming
close to Jesus Christ.

One is often asked—by Christians who are trying to
test the ' orthodoxy ' of the speaker, or by non-Christians
who are trying to gauge his tolerant comprehensiveness—
what one thinks will be the fate of the ' heathen ' (their
word, not mine). The reply is that no man will be
finally condemned until he has had the opportunity of

[1] I am indebted for this summary to Bishop Henry Read, formerly of
Nasik, who tells me that it came from a Marathi translation of the original
Hindi.

seeing God in Christ, without any possibility of misunderstanding. Somewhere in this life or in the next,
every man will see Christ, as he really is, not through the
words or life of any individual which could so easily
mislead him, but in direct spiritual vision and experience.

To man there remain eternally two ways. And the
one that is crowded is still the one that leads to destruction ; and many there be that find it. But at
some point on that road, be it far or near, each one
finds also something, or rather Someone, else. It is a
figure stooping beneath the weight of a cross. ' Lord,
where are you going ? ' asks Everyman. And the
answer comes : ' I am going to Rome, to Moscow, to
New York, to be crucified afresh in your place.' And
no man in the end can bear that encounter for ever ;
for it is an encounter with a Power than which there
can be nothing greater, a meeting with omnipotent
Love itself. This love will take no man's choice from
him ; for it is precisely his choice that it wants.[1]

PRAYERS

O ETERNAL WORD,
    who from the beginning hast revealed
    glimpses of truth and righteousness
    through prophets of many faiths,
        we praise thee
    that all that is of value
    is found fulfilled and perfected in thee,
    and all that is mistaken
    finds its correction
        in thee.
Do thou draw all seekers of truth and righteousness
        to thyself,
and vouchsafe to them the unsearchable riches
    that can be found in thee alone.

                              G. A.

[1] J. A. T. Robinson, *In the End, God* . . . (James Clarke & Co.)

O Spirit of God, guide me as I seek to discover thy working with men of other faiths. Give me the strength of truth, the gentleness and strength of love, the clear eye of judgment and the courage of faith. Above all, grant me a deeper understanding of him who is the Truth, a greater commitment to him who is the Lord, a deeper gratitude to him who is the Saviour of all, even Jesus Christ thy Eternal Word, through them thou art drawing all men to thyself, that they may be saved for ever, and worship thee the only true God blessed for evermore.

G. A.

O Lord and Saviour Christ, Who camest not to strive nor cry, but to let thy words fall as the drops that water the earth ; grant all who contend for the Faith once delivered, never to injure it by clamour and impatience ; but speaking thy precious Truth in Love so to present it that it may be loved, and that men may see in it thy goodness and thy beauty ; Who livest and reignest with the Father and the Holy Spirit, one God world without end.

W. Bright

CHAPTER VII

THE LOVE OF CHRIST

IT is said that when S. John was a very old man all that
he could or would say to those who came to see the last
surviving apostle of Jesus was, ' Little children, love one
another.' In his Gospel he had recorded this as the Lord's
last command to his disciples and had given it an inex-
haustible content which men could never live up to
unless Christ were in them to enable them to do so. ' A
new commandment I give unto you, that ye love one
another, *as I have loved you.*' By the time S. John wrote
his epistle it was an old commandment to the disciple
whom Jesus loved, but it was still new to new converts.
The second commandment in the Law, ' Thou shalt love
thy neighbour as thyself,' is left far behind : now we must
love one another with the love with which Christ loves us.

If we are to win people to Christ it will be only through a
love that in some way tells them or reminds them of Christ's
love. ' On the closing pages of the Gospels there is con-
tained what we might not inaptly describe as an examination
paper to test proficiency in discipleship. It consists of but
three questions, and they are all alike : "Lovest thou me?"
Christianity can only do its perfect work in us as we set ourselves to learn the lesson of absolute Devotion to our Lord.' [1]

Our Lord demands that our love for him shall be the
chief thing in our lives, so far beyond all other loves that
it might seem to people who do not know him that we
are almost hating others. ' He that loveth father or
mother more than me is not worthy of me.' ' If any man
come to me, and hate not his father, and mother, and wife,

---

[1] A. W. Robinson, *The Personal Life of the Clergy* (Longmans)

and children, and brethren, and sisters, yea, and his own
life also, he cannot be my disciple.' There could hardly be
stronger language than this. But given the right love to
Christ all other loves fall into their proper place and become
greater loves than merely human loving can produce.

How can we gain that love for him? First of all, it
will spring from the consciousness of his love to us :
' God so loved the world that he gave his Son '. Christ so
loved the world that he gave his life, ' God commendeth
his love toward us in that while we were yet sinners
Christ died for us ', ' the Son of God who loved me, and
gave himself up for me '. The New Testament lights up
from page to page with mentions of the love of God-in-
Christ. ' We love him,' says S. John, ' because he first
loved us.' As little children we learnt love from our
parents : love was awakened in us as a response to their
love. So love for Christ will awaken in our hearts, as we
study the love of Christ revealed in the Gospel pages.

> Let him be thy model
>   for thy every word and deed,
> moving or standing,
>   seated, eating,
>   silent or speaking,
>   alone or with others.
>   Study him
> and thou wilt grow in his love,
>   in his company
> thou wilt gain sweetness and confidence
> and thou wilt be strengthened in every virtue.
>   Let this be thy wisdom
>   this thy meditation
>   this thy study
>   to have him always in mind
>   to move thee to imitation
>   to win thee to his love.[1]

[1] Archbishop Goodier, *The Light that is Life* (Burns, Oates and Wash-
bourne Ltd.)

The second way of learning love is to realize the in-dwelling Christ. S. Paul prays for his Ephesian converts in a way that makes this clear : ' I bow my knees unto the Father . . . that he would grant you, according to the riches of his glory, to be strengthened with might by his Spirit in the inner man ; that Christ may dwell in your hearts by faith ; that ye, being rooted and grounded in love, may be able to comprehend with all saints what is the breadth, and length, and depth, and height ; and to know the love of Christ, which passeth knowledge, that ye might be filled with all the fulness of God.'

If Christ is in us, his love will be there with him ; he loves us, we shall love him in return ; he will love through us, so we shall love our fellow men. The test of our love for him will be whether or not we love others. S. John, the apostle of love can be very scathing : ' If a man say, I love God, and hateth his brother, he is a liar.' If Christ is truly in us, we shall love the other man as ' the brother for whom Christ died '. If we give help or refuse help to others, it will be as if we did it or did it not unto Christ.

When we take our part in Christ's mission to the world, love will be the hallmark of our participation. ' Woe is unto me, if I preach not the Gospel ' : true, but ' if I speak with the tongues of men and of angels and have not love, I am become as sounding brass, or a clanging cymbal.' We can love men into the Kingdom of God, even if we cannot preach them into it. This means a new attitude to the Buddhist or the Muslim or the Hindu or the simple animist or the Communist, who claims he is god-less. It is a very wholesome thing for the missionary to ask himself, ' How many Buddhists do I love ? . . . Is there even one Buddhist whom I have loved ? ' Or for the preacher, who so strongly and unfailingly denounces Communism, to count up the number of Communists with whom he has made friends. Often the man who claims to be an atheist is not really godless : he may be an honest agnostic who can only say that he does not know, or he may be only rejecting the God we offer, ' our God ', not the God and Father of Jesus Christ. ' Our God ' may be far too small ; he may be looking for the living God whom he fails to recognize in our preaching and living.

If God made every man, if God loves every man, if Christ died for every man, he will be somewhere around every man. ' The fruit of the Spirit is love,' says S. Paul, and if God is the source of love, then the converse must be true : where love is, God is, as Tolstoy entitled one of his stories. Wherever there is love, wherever there is truth, there God is ; let us gladly recognize his presence, even if other people's eyes do not penetrate further than recognition of love and truth. If God created man, then the love of man and wife, parent and child, friend and friend, was implanted by him. Let us start simply and gladly with the recognition of human love and trace it back patiently to its source. And wherever love is expressed towards that which men count as God, let us not doubt that the God of love will accept it and reveal more of himself to those who love. Study these expressions of love :

1. O my Lord ! If I worship thee from fear of hell, burn me in hell : and if I worship thee from hope of paradise, exclude me thence ; but if I worship thee for thine own sake, then withhold not from me thine eternal beauty.

2. Now may every living thing, feeble or strong, omitting none, or tall or middle-sized or short, subtle or gross of form, seen or unseen, dwelling near or far away, born or yet unborn, may every living thing be full of bliss.

3. From the beginning until the end of time there

is love between me and thee, and how shall such love be extinguished ?

4.   This is my prayer to thee, my Lord—strike, strike at the root of penury in my heart.

Give me the strength lightly to bear my joys and sorrows.

Give me the strength to make my love fruitful in service.

Give me the strength never to disown the poor or bend my knees before insolent might.

Give me the strength to raise my mind high above daily trifles.

And give me the strength to surrender my strength to thy will with love.[1]

All these four prayers come from non-Christians : the first from Rābi'ah, a Muslim woman mystic who lived about A.D. 800 ; the second is said to go back to the Buddha ; the third comes from Kabir, a Hindu weaver and mystic of the fifteenth century ; and the last comes from Rabindranath Tagore, who died in 1941. Can we doubt that the Spirit of God breathes in these prayers or that they are acceptable unto the living God, the Creator and Saviour of all ? Wherever we find love, truth, spiritual depth, let us reverently acknowledge that the Lord is there, waiting perhaps for our loving service before his hidden presence can be manifested in all his love and glory.

In all our witness we must be as humble as the Lord of Bethlehem and Calvary, as unfailingly loving as he. Early in my missionary service I was given an unexpected lesson in the humility of language. In Burmese you can say the words ' I, you ' in four different ways : the first pair are appropriate to an older or senior person speaking to a younger or junior man ; the second denote equality between the speaker and the person to

---

[1] Rabindranath Tagore, *Gitanjali* (Macmillan)

whom he is talking ; the third are used by a human being speaking to an animal or addressing a criminal or worthless person ; the fourth by an inferior person speaking to his master or a pupil to his teacher. An interpreter would invariably set the speaker on the highest level, and the missionary proficient in the language would have to be persistent in his use of the humbler words before he could persuade his hearers that he had deliberately chosen these words and was not just being an ignorant novice in the use of language. Our prayer must be to be as humble as Christ ; we cannot be more humble, for he has gone to the lowest depths and has sat down in the lowest place. ' I am among you as he that serveth.'

The Christian Church has not always served Christ in humble and loving service. This is seen particularly in its treatment of the Jews or in its acquiescence in persecution of the Jews all down the centuries since the crucifixion. Between Christians and Jews lie 1,900 years of wrong treatment, of persecution, forced conversion, expulsion, ostracism, anti-semitism. The result has been that the Jew cannot see Christ because of Christian history ; he cannot get to Christ because he is thronged by Christians who seem so unlike him.

Rabbi Leo Baeck, a modern Jew who was in close touch with Christians, was emphatic that in its approach to the Jewish religion it was not only the content of the Church's message that mattered, but the manner in which it was presented. ' The style is the man, and one could emphatically add : the religion too.'

Christians are in the habit of speaking of the Jews as the people who crucified Jesus Christ, and thus marking them off from all other races. The more one studies the records of the Passion and the more one learns about happenings in totalitarian countries, the more clearly one can see that it was a cleverly and ruthlessly organized plot which resulted in the Crucifixion. Preachers often

compare the fickleness of the Jewish crowd which could
shout ' Hosanna ' on Palm Sunday and ' Crucify him ' on
Good Friday. The fact is that they were different
crowds : the crowd on Palm Sunday was composed
largely of pilgrims from Galilee who knew and loved
Jesus, together with some ordinary interested people of
Jerusalem, while the crowd on Good Friday was an
organized crowd got together by a political party and
carefully prepared what and when to shout. Jews were
undoubtedly the instigators of the plot, but let us not
forget that we Gentiles were represented in the person of
Pontius Pilate who, convinced of the innocence of the
prisoner before him, gave in to organized political
pressure, while Gentile soldiers were the instruments of
both a weak governor and political fanatics. Jews and
Gentiles, we both stand guilty before the Cross of Jesus
Christ ; both are equally saved by it. A recognition of
the involvement of all men in Calvary could help the
Jew to feel that he has not been made the scapegoat of
the world's greatest tragedy, in which, however, by the
power of God utmost evil was turned into highest blessing.

Kenneth Cragg in *The Call of the Minaret*, a most sig-
nificant book in this time of new encounter, speaks of the
bitter traditions in the Middle East of the Crusades,
which were for centuries looked upon by the Church as
a glorious episode, but are now being recognized as a
tragedy of misguided devotion. ' The Crusades,' he
says, ' were served with a devotion that, had it been as
wise and true as it was fervent and undaunted, would
have blessed the Eastern world.' As it was, they revealed
a mistaken idea that Christ's concern was for sacred
places and not for souls. ' The gain of Jerusalem had no
merit to supplant the giving of Christ. The Crusades
were a mistaken gesture of a disloyal Christendom.' [1]

Yet Francis of Assisi insisted on trying the way of love

[1] Kenneth Cragg, *The Call of the Minaret* (Oxford University Press)

and went unarmed into Saladin's camp to preach the love of Christ. A prayer of his that has come down to us may well have been prayed in that adventure of love :

> Lord, make us instruments of thy peace.
>> Where there is hatred, let us sow love ;
>> where there is injury, pardon ;
>> where there is discord, union ;
>> where there is doubt, faith ;
>> where there is despair, hope ;
>> where there is darkness, light ;
>> where there is sadness, joy ;
>>> for thy mercy and for thy truth's sake.

Another apostle of love of the thirteenth century was Raymond Lull, who ' saw many knights going to the Holy Land, thinking they can acquire it by force of arms.' He recognized that ' he who loves not, lives not ' and that the only way to win the world is by ' the pouring out of tears and blood.'

A more modern example of one who tried to serve his Muslim brethren in love was Charles de Foucauld. He began life as a French soldier and served with great distinction in North Africa. Becoming converted to Christ he joined a Trappist order, but later went back to the Sahara to serve the people there as a hermit, only to be murdered in 1916 after many years of loving service. Two of his sayings sum up the heart of missionary service : ' All men without any exception are my brethren, I am the universal brother ', and ' I want to shout the Gospel with my whole life.'

' I am the universal brother '—brother to all who are trying to find religious truth, brother to all who are trying to live the good life, brother to men in their sufferings, their failures and their sins, brother to men in their lovings and longings, because Christ came to be a brother to me and to show me the way to the Father's home.

A continental scholar recently wrote a history of the early years of the British missionary movement. With sensitive insight and generous appreciation he entitled his study, *Constrained by Jesus' Love*. The outstanding men and women in our modern missionary history were people of love : Thomas Bray with his care for the English settlers overseas ; John Wesley with his conviction of the saving love of Christ, taking the whole world as his parish ; William Carey with his insistence that our Lord's commission to his disciples was binding on Christians in all generations, together with his concern for the widows of India which resulted in the abolition of their burning in *suttee* ; Wilberforce and the Venns in their love of the slaves ; Henry Martyn burning himself out for God ; Alexander Duff with his love of the students in India ; Livingstone with his love of the Africans ; Frank Weston with an equally burning love and a hatred of all injustice ; Mary Slessor the matriarch of Calabar ; Gladys Aylward with her heroic care of Chinese orphans in our own time. All these latter-day saints and countless others showed Christ's love in their presentation of the Gospel in word and in life. They were loving enough to present Christ with urgency and with an appeal for commitment.

We, who believe that there are pointers in the great religions to the Eternal Christ and that there are truths and values in them which are fulfilled and perfected in him, also know that sooner or later commitment is called for. A new birth has to be accepted involving a break with the past. Every converted Christian, whether he comes from a non-Christian past or a nominally Christian background, knows of this leap of faith by which he casts himself at the feet of Christ as Lord and Saviour.

Convinced as we are of Christ's love for men living or departed, and confident as we are that every man shall at some point know and understand God's Last Word to men, yet there must be a note of urgency about our presentation of the Gospel. A day without Christ is a day lost. Men must not be left to live without Christ or die without Christ. We must help them to see him as relevant in every situation, personal, social and international, as gospel to every religion, the same yesterday and today and for ever, yet becoming more wonderful every day that we follow him. He still comes to seek and to save, and when men come to him, they realize that he has always been pursuing them, though they did not recognize him. And we who have known him will speak gratefully and lovingly of what he has done, as someone infinitely dear to us whom we want them to know. We know of no other name by which men can be saved ; having known him we should be lost without him.

> None other Lamb, none other Name,
>   None other Hope in heaven or earth or sea,
> None other Hiding-place from guilt and shame,
>   None beside Thee.
>
> My faith burns low, my hope burns low
>   Only my heart's desire cries out in me
> By the deep thunder of its want and woe
>   Cries out to Thee.
>
> Lord, Thou art Life tho' I be dead,
>   Love's Fire Thou art, however cold I be :
> Nor heaven have I, nor place to lay my head,
>   Nor home, but Thee. [1]

PRAYERS

GIVE us grace, O God our Father, to keep this day and always the new commandment and the great commandment and all the commandments, by loving

[1] By Christina Georgina Rosetti

thee with all our mind and soul and strength, and one
another for thy sake ; in the name of Jesus Christ
our Lord.

E. Milner-White

ALMIGHTY and everlasting God, who hast willed
to restore all things in Thy well-beloved Son, the
King and Lord of all : mercifully grant that all
peoples and nations, divided and wounded by sin,
may be brought under the gentle yoke of His most
loving rule ; Who with Thee and the Holy Spirit
liveth and reigneth, ever one God, world without end.

Sarum

O GOD our Judge and Saviour, set before us the
vision of Thy purity, and let us see our sins in the light
of Thy countenance ; pierce our self-contentment
with the shafts of Thy burning love and let that love
consume in us all that hinders us from perfect service
of Thy cause ; for as Thy holiness is our judgment,
so are Thy wounds our salvation.

William Temple

Worthy of praise from every mouth,
    of confession from every tongue,
    of worship from every creature,
is thy glorious Name, O Father, Son and Holy Ghost ;
    who didst create the world in thy grace
    and by thy compassion didst save the world.

Nestorian Liturgy

SUGGESTIONS FOR MEDITATION
AND DISCUSSION

Chapter 1

1. How would you explain your reasons for believing in God to a Buddhist from Burma or Ceylon, or to someone who does not believe in God?

2. Every Christian ought to be able to say something of his own experience of God. How would you express yours?

3. How has man's discovery of nuclear energy and his achievement in putting satellites round the sun made any difference to your faith in God as Creator?

Chapter 2

1. What would you reply to a man who says that he can accept Christ as the greatest teacher who ever lived, but he cannot accept him as Lord and God?

2. C. F. Andrews, one of the most loved missionaries to India, wrote a book with the title, *What I Owe to Christ*. What would be the main points if you were to write such a book?

3. How far can we expect people of other faiths to accept the Christian doctrine of the Trinity before they have accepted Christ as Lord?

Chapter 3

1. ' If any man is in Christ he is a new creature.' Think out the change which Christ has made in your own life and look for further changes which he may be wanting you to make.

2. How would you explain to a non-Christian friend the difference which Christ has made in your interpretation of death?

3. It is not sufficient for the individual to be converted to Christ, he must also work for the new order of the Kingdom of God. Mention ways in which the Christian Church is trying to do this in the world to-day.

Chapter 4

1. The Holy Spirit has been described as the Unknown God. What has the Bible to say about the Holy Spirit and what he does?

2. The Holy Spirit is ' God in men '. What reasons would you give to a Hindu friend to help him understand that the Spirit of God lives and works in men but must not be identified with the spirit of man?

3. How can we make it possible for the Holy Spirit to cleanse and sanctify the deepest levels of personality?

Chapter 5

1. How is your Church ' considering its relation to other Churches in the light of our Lord's prayer that we may be sanctified in the truth and that we may all be one '?

2. How can your congregation be ' a true family of God, where every man can find a home and know that God loves him without limit '?

3. How do you express your concern that today when the Church of Christ is a world-wide fellowship there are countless people to whom he is unknown?

4. ' Does your congregation live for itself, or for the world around it and beyond it ? ' [1]

Chapter 6

1. ' To the Muslim I became as a Muslim. To the Buddhist I became as a Buddhist. To the Hindu I became as a Hindu.' How far is it possible for the Christian to do this?

2. ' Christ stands as the judge of all religion.' What things are there in our contemporary expression of Christianity, either as denominations or as local congregations, that would have to plead ' Guilty ' before him?

3. ' We do not want to convert you to us, not even to the best of us.' What is it that we want to do?

[1] Based on questions from *Evanston Speaks*, Reports from the Second Assembly of the World Council of Churches, August 15–31, 1954, published for the World Council of Churches by S.C.M. Press, London.